KT-568-971

Parenting the sh*t out of life

Parenting the sh*t out of life

For people who happen to be parents (or might be soon).

Mother Pukka.

(Anna Whitehouse)

Papa Pukka.

(Matt Farquharson)

HODDER &
STOUGHTON

First published in Great Britain in 2017 by Hodder & Stoughton
An Hachette UK company

7

Picture credits: Icons (p. 54) – mints, pot noodle © Matt Hodgson; golf tee ©
Iconic Bestiary/Shutterstock; aerosol, ketchup packet © vectorisland/
Shutterstock; condom © Gel00/Shutterstock; can, memory stick © Rvector/
Shutterstock; pencil © Victor Metelskiy/Shutterstock; train ticket ©
BesticonPark/Shutterstock, phone © Anya Ku/Shutterstock, handheld console
© VectorsMarket/Shutterstock, trainer © kosmofish/Shutterstock. Illustrations
(p. 153) – Tamagotchi toy © Yorri/Shutterstock; baby © Saphatthachat
Sunchoote/Shutterstock. Taxidermy – p. 257: © Johner Images/Getty, ©
travelib environment / Alamy; p. 258: © WENN Ltd / Alamy; p. 259: ©
WENN Ltd / Alamy; p. 260: © WENN Ltd / Alamy Stock Photo.

A CIP catalogue record for this title is
available from the British Library

ISBN 978 1 473 66576 7
eBook ISBN 978 1 473 66578 1
Tradepaperback ISBN 978 1 473 66908 6

Typeset in ITC Mendoza by Palimpsest Book Production Ltd,
Falkirk, Stirlingshire

Printed and bound by CPI Group (UK) Ltd, Croydon, CR0 4YY

Hodder & Stoughton policy is to use papers that are natural, renewable
and recyclable products and made from wood grown in sustainable forests.
The logging and manufacturing processes are expected to conform to
the environmental regulations of the country of origin.

Hodder & Stoughton Ltd
Carmelite House
50 Victoria Embankment
London EC4Y 0DZ

www.hodder.co.uk

To Mae and Eve. And to all the mamas, papas, grannies, grandads, aunties, uncles and the mates who hold the baby while you have a wee. Here's to working on life.

Contents

Introduction

Mother Pukka.

Parenting, eh. It's a word that deeply concerned me until I was about twenty-eight. It was associated with grim, bulging nappies in public toilets and Mars-bar-smattered kids flicking bogeys at your hungover head. It didn't look like a happy place. Those parents didn't look like happy people – not like the faux ones in John Lewis picture frames.

I took my contraceptive pill with military scheduling.

Then I met a boy who wasn't a bell-end and wanted his seed in a way that I believe only David Attenborough can fully explain: 'Here we have the primitive female on the procreational turn . . .'

That seed turned into Mae – part boombox, part wonderful human – and we went from happy to nappy place. The full show: eye-twitching sleepless nights, leaking mammaries, living off your kid's cold, discarded fish fingers (tramp canapés as a mate refers to them). But while Sellotaping my life together post-splashdown, I remember thinking it's not a complete horror show.

Sure it leaves your fun bags resembling a spaniel's ears and your mind a little mangled. But those moments when you catch a gurning toothless smile; or when you get a little hand-squeeze in response to your own; or when you manage to have a wee – complete with closed door, without a toddler gawping at you – those are the bits that make you think, 'Yeah, we're working on life here, people.'

It's a tale of two halves: one minute you're sauntering with your stroller, kid asleep, weekly shop tucked under the buggy, owning life. The next you're trying to manhandle a planking toddler into a buggy as an entire bus stop of blue-rinsed ladies quietly judge. It's at this point that a rogue grape usually rolls from your protruding bag into a gutter – the final embellishment on that shitty parental cake.

Mother Fucker! There it is. An expletive is uttered in a very British way (so no one can hear), and I'm left looking like I've escaped from an institution. So remember, the next time you see a mother angrily grumbling in the rain and trying to 'parent', you'll understand the truth behind her mutterings.

However, my own mum hates swearing, so when I decided to set out on a mission to blather about the good, bad and ugly of parenting online it was 'Mother Pukka' that made the cut. The aim was to bring all those offspring-avoiders into the nook and help parents (and parents-to-be) understand that we're all doing better than we think. With brutally honest anecdotes, the purpose of Mother Pukka is to share what it really takes to build and raise a human.

It is based on a ratio of laughing more than you cry. It is a pixelated hug for the mother who is postnatally depressed, feeding a mewling infant at 3 a.m. only to hear a bunch of youths coming back from a night on the tiles as a stark reminder of another far-off world. It is hopefully a 'me too' place when parents find themselves standing in Tesco with a shrieking child, a pineapple and one solitary tear edging down their face, unsure of how to proceed with this spiky, exotic fruit.

The ambition of Mother Pukka is to offer some light relief from that stain-embellished, madly brilliant parental storm. My feeling is that however you choose to parent – eco-warrior or plastic-purchaser, gym-bunny or gin-bunny, hipster dad or hip-replacement dad – the common denominator is humour. If we can laugh through the madness as we keep those small humans alive, then we truly are winning.

This book is an extension of Mother Pukka, a bosomy, welcoming place for people who happen to be parents, or for people who are about to become parents, and our motto is: 'parenting the shit out of life'. Because, for every turdy nappy you sadly deposit into a gag-reflex-inducing bin, there's a moment that's less shit around the corner. A moment when your life project says, 'Mama has a spiky hoo-ha' in the tinned goods aisle of your local supermarket and you realise that you're laughing more than you're crying.

Here's to parenting the shit out of life.

Papa Pukka.

There are no parenting books that tell you what to do when your child starts to squawk and thrash about like a pterodactyl in a tumble dryer. There's no manual that clarifies whether it's okay secretly to eat your nipper's last fruit pastille, or advises on the best response to accidentally being peed on while pretending to be a pony. These are things you learn as you go along, because every parent is winging it.

Every mama and papa becomes a multi-talented improviser who can shift from surrealist clown to concerned guardian in the time it takes to fall off a swing. This is not a guidebook or a philosophy. It is not designed to guilt you into signing up to a parenting style. It's a list of things that happened, some of which might also happen to you. (Apart from the bit about having a beagle that ingests heroin. That's unlikely to happen to anyone else.)

I used to have big dreams; now I have big bags under my eyes. Where once I dreamt of writing a great, British novel, scoring a World-Cup-final hat-trick or becoming the country's finest-ever Prime Minister, now I dream of uninterrupted sleep and a day when no one in my house cries. I used to enjoy hangovers because they allowed me to lie in and plan elaborate breakfasts. Now I am hungover every day, regardless of whether or not I've drunk the night before.

I have voluntarily imposed these minor agonies on myself because I was vain enough to think that the world needed more of me, and decided to have a child. That child – our strident, loving, funny, caring, selfish, generous, curious, fragile, bold and brave four-year-old daughter – has changed my life in all the ways you might expect, and in many others that came as a complete surprise. One of the most significant was realising that I lived with something called a 'vlogger'.

Anna began Mother Pukka for Mae. She had built a career as a journalist over ten years, but when the money and hours proved incompatible with parenting – about which, more later – she took a job as senior copywriter for L'Oreal Group. It paid more, but the hours were still long. With me doing the childcare drop-off in the morning, Anna could make pick-up by 5.59 p.m., giving her an hour with Mae each evening. Then L'Oreal's office moved and her daily commute went from ninety minutes to two and half hours, meaning she would only see Mae sleeping and at weekends. Something had to give, and Mother Pukka was born.

Two years into our parenting experiment, she began spending every spare moment with her nose to her mobile: blogging, vlogging, Instagramming and pouring her time in to Mother Pukka. It was an explosion of curiosity, creativity and rage about the unnecessary impossibilities of modern parenting. While I was griping about childcare costs and the lack of flexible employment, she was speaking up for like-minded parents by organising dancing flash-mobs in Trafalgar Square. While I grizzled about the preachy nature of most parenting guides and an industry aimed at guilt-tripping, Anna had quit her job to hold forth from a very colourful digital soapbox, standing up to say: 'It's okay guys, we're all working on life.'

This is simply a way of saying: parenting is tough, and the expectations on this generation of parents are making it tougher than it needs to be. There are some little boxes throughout this book that offer practical tips, but mostly parenting is more intuitive than you might think. Things go wrong, everyone mucks up, but when the time comes, you'll work it out. Just be patient, be kind and show your kids interesting things. Make them eat some vegetables and brush most of their teeth. Don't let them be twats to others. And when it gets tricky, speak to a few trusted friends. If you've picked up this book, then you've probably just made or are brewing (or are considering brewing) an actual human, which is about the most amazing thing anyone can do. The next two decades will be tough, but don't worry: you've got this.

Here's to parenting the shit out of life.

DISCLAIMER

Like most parents, we're making it up as we go along. Our main sources of advice are 'friends who look like they're holding it together', the internet and fleeting instincts. This book is meant to make you laugh a bit and is not a substitute for professional advice.

1

The years BC*

*before child

Mother Pukka.

Lying is a strong word.

'I'm just not sure I want to get married or have babies,' I coolly lilted on a post-bender comedown, while watching the twenty-third episode of *The Sopranos*. I remember feeling vaguely cool: I was in my boyfriend's 'travelling' T-shirt – he'd worn it on a cardboard-cut-out gap year around the world, which AMAZED me – and I had a 'creative' Moleskine notebook full of lists that said things like, 'Call Grandma'. I also had a nose-piercing, the symbol of the anti-family. I was 'breezy'.

We ordered a pizza (stuffed crust). We ate it in bed – post-bonk pizza crumbs in the bed are the pinnacle of twenties success – and the very thought of anyone, or anything, mewling its way into that fun-pit was a little south of acceptable. My boyfriend, Matt, thought he'd cashed in a twenty-first-century fembot, complete with an above-average blowie technique. The years stretched ahead of us as a veritable Disneyland of fun and carefree frolics, embellished with a steady flow of hangover-easing Gregg's sausage rolls.

Now, a little bit more about The Breezy Friendly Girl (The BFG). She owns a casually beaten – read: manufactured to look that way – faux-leather biker jacket and drinks black filter coffee despite knowing it tastes like bitter soil infused with Campari. In her mind she likes Scandi stuff while hiding grot reads such as *Now* and the occasional well-thumbed Mills & Boon in her bag. In her mind she's a chubbier version of girl-next-door Holly Willoughboobie with a dash of class A's for good measure. She eats Monster Munch but imagines she lives off puréed kale, and she doesn't succumb to snotty-nosed emotional breakdowns. She travels to Prague for, like, cultural reasons but always ends up absinthed to the eyeballs in some Euro trash gaff.

The reality of The BFG is that she was working as a junior reporter on *Practical Caravan Magazine* – as the tow-bar expert – having been cruelly rejected by Saatchi & Saatchi. (They rejected me on a graduate pitch where I put forward my dog-walking business, named Doggy Style. Their loss.)

I aspired to have perfectly manicured nails at every waking moment but was often looking down at Biro-stained stubs. I would never have my Oyster card ready at the Tube barrier, to the overwhelming irk of The People of London, and was quietly delighted by terrible advertising puns like 'gimme, gimme, gimme a naan after midnight'. I was someone who cultivated a world of sodden receipts at the bottom of my bag – from bars, restaurants and all manner of confectionery extravagances – but would never delve too deep for fear of what lies beneath.

But The BFG is not always as she seems and Mother Nature is – as we know from the maternal hamsters that snack on their young – a wily mistress. She giveth and taketh without a care for the baffled male life-forms in her path: one minute you're rocking out in a mosh pit, the next you're Googling ovulation cycles. Over those three years I'd spent with Matt, I'd hidden any desire for marriage and babies with breeziness. A faux breeziness is a terrifying thing. It's all coat-hanger smiles and overwhelming smugness about 'how happy we are just the two of us; we're different; we don't need those bulging, sodden nappies in our lives; and let's just spend the money on a snazzy coffee machine'.

But then the mates start getting hitched. You get asked to be a bridesmaid and you see some other bristly-faced man stand up and tell the world how ace his lobster is. Then another comes along – this time your best friend – and you live every minute of that wedding (almost to the detriment of your friendship; but all harmony is restored five years later), and you see the possibilities. What was once a turgid occasion becomes 'just a big party for all your mates'. What's so wrong with that?

Your breeziness starts to edge into disgruntled waters as you get moist in the eye over insurance adverts depicting two hamsters looking after each other 'in sickness and in health'. They just seem to care so much; what's a little marital branding when the rodent-love is that deep? Perhaps then you realise it's time to unleash the marital cattle prod.

The BFG has been swept away by a gust of wind. She's scarpered into the hills with bulging Pinterest boards in her wake. She doesn't even like a stuffed crust any more. What a brave new world. Babies? How cool would that be? A small version of yourself running around; what's not to love? What's the big deal? It's just a party for god's sakes! Chill your boots: I want it all and I want it now.

Cue Douglas the flatulent beagle. I felt at this confusing juncture, we needed an excitable canine in our lives. Matt thought it would buy him some time before the marriage and babies, but I saw it as a parental training exercise. Douglas came home with us and he was our first foray into keeping something alive and wiping up shit that wasn't ours. Douglas is a hound with a backstory: he was from a rescue centre and had been found living on the streets of Antwerp (we lived in Amsterdam at the time) – he was obese, so he had clearly been successful in his endeavours. It was survival of the fattest and he had a hunger like no other.

Within three hours of getting him home from the rescue centre, it was clear we had made a catastrophic mistake. This was no pooch who would snuggle up at your feet in some gastropub as you casually read the Sunday papers. We invited mates round for dinner that weekend and as we opened the door to let them in, Douglas had mounted the table and face-planted a bowl of Wotsits. He raised his head with an orange, crumb moustache as our open-minded friends quietly judged our ability to dog-parent. The dog was ON the dining table. He was adventurous. Then there was the terrifying event post-

Amsterdam's Gay Pride where people were abandoning condoms on the street willy-nilly – I still can't talk about what I had to wrestle from his salivating jaw.

So there we were, living above a retailer called 'The Happy Sex Shop' in Amsterdam's red-light district. The window downstairs often had DVDs of someone who looked worryingly like my Aunty Julie, doing implausible things with legumes. I'll never forget the series: 'My First Cucumber' then 'My First Aubergine' and finally 'My First Marrow' . . . a horticultural masterpiece. And then one evening, a baffled-as-a-badger-in-the-headlights Matt observed me crumple in front of the dishwasher – with the smell of congealed ketchup in the air – and warble 'Why won't you marry meeeeee?' through snot bubbles and black tears. (Mascara is not a merry match for the saddened.)

How that gargantuan U-turn came about is unclear even to me. I suppose, to the outside world, the three years previous to it could resemble the movements of a black widow spider. Lurking with marital intent behind that little trapdoor, waiting for the moment to pounce and demand a fucking massive rock and all the pastel-hued (irrelevant but essential) wedding trimmings. The truth is I'm just more socially organised than Matt and we both had the same feelings, simply a different timescale.

But ultimately I wanted him. I wanted him for ever, and then – to the genuine confusion of Douglas the beagle, who had been watching our exchange, wide-eyed from a corner – Matt halted my torrent of distressed emotion with the words:

'I fucking love you; of course I want to marry you. I was just going to do it in Greece on a hilltop next month.'

Greece would have been much nicer than next to the dishwasher. What a prune. But there we were, engaged, standing above The Happy Sex Shop with only a bemused, relentlessly farting beagle to share the giddy news with.

'Cup of tea?'

'Yeah, okay.'

The poor man was in too deep to pull a swift U-ey. I'd called my mum and she had a venue nailed down by nightfall; the woman takes to a challenge like no other. There was talk of us getting married in six months. Matt nervously laughed: 'Okay, let's just rip the plaster off!'

My engagement ring was swiftly bought for £3.50 from a ring dispenser outside a prostitute's window – the rings were meant to be bought by punters for their favourite ladies of the night. The tagline merrily said: 'Do a nice thing, buy her a ring!' It seemed befitting.

Looking back, I'd never communicated the shift of marital neediness to Matt. He was still in those heady days where the only focus was on his own happy ending. I'd drop hints: 'Ah, it's so cool that James and Alice are getting married – they're such a great couple . . . married after just two years, amazing!' I'd give whimsical, longing looks at him during wedding speeches, even if what was being said was emotional guff. There would be a hand-squeeze here, a deep staring into his confused, often-vacant eyes there. Nothing explicit, just hints that seemed transparent, clear and obvious.

I wanted him to shit or get off the pot and felt that three years of my finest relationship work (with knockers at their perky peak) was enough to push the reluctant Scot over the threshold. He'd had my best years and he was going to seal this with a snog at the altar.

I am doing myself a little disservice here; I'm not some poisonous arachnid or screaming banshee with a procreational clock thudding away in the background. I just harboured a deep love for the man who still to this day puts his socks bundled up into the washing machine so that they come out sodden knots of cloth. I love him, through sickness and in health – despite the sock balls.

It was around this point that he affectionately started calling me 'Cum Pot', which I didn't flinch at. I just thought the contract we were entering into was so clear. It was only a few years later that I remarked how funny it was he called me that and he said: 'The fruit, a kumquat; I was referring to you as a lovely little tropical fruit.'

After the proposal I was delighted to be able to launch my Pinterest work fully. If Matt was ever concerned about my state of mind, he didn't show it – he's a trooper and a really nice man. A flood of peonies, porcelain puppies and other shit we didn't need was unleashed into the domestic arena. Full wed-min had commenced. He once showed a flicker of interest in our choice of table favours – until he realised we weren't talking about crisp 'flavours' (he wanted Prawn Cocktail if it was a genuine discussion). We lost him in the abundance of unnecessary off-white paraphernalia.

The wedding was a little teaser of what was to come: Project Procreation. On our wedding night I was determined to get some action out of my lobster and seal the deal on our newfound, marital happiness. In reality, I awoke in full Agent Provocateur finery (purchased the day before, rather awkwardly, with my dad at the Bicester Village outlet), with a Lindt chocolate ball in my belly button.

The inclusion of chocolate had seemed overwhelmingly sexual at the time. I had rampant visions of him nibbling that little confection before humping our way into the next morning. But I had passed out, and when I woke I'd forgotten all about the molten treat and thought I'd crapped myself. Devastation doesn't cover it; no bride wants to wake up to accidental defecation. I like to think that moment solidified us as a couple – forget consummating the marriage, try navigating a bed-shitting incident without any finger-pointing. He's my rock – but we will never eat another Lindt ball so long as we both shall live.

The honeymoon wasn't to be the holidaying pinnacle of our lives. A few days into our Vietnamese meander, I read a Facebook post about one of my best mates, which read: 'RIP babes, so sorry to hear this.'

I frantically trawled the internet, emailing friends, messaging people in a blind panic to see what that rogue 'RIP' was doing there. I couldn't see straight and was striding about the compound we were staying in, flitting between 'no one would write that, it's a joke' to 'what the fuck, what the fuck, what the fuck'.

But the devastating truth surfaced that one of my best friends, Toni, had killed herself two days after our wedding. My friend Dave said everyone tried to keep it from us, so we wouldn't hear while away on honeymoon. I was broken, numb, dreaming of her in fleeting, elusive moments of sleep, wondering how I had been consumed with a glorified party and not seen the signs of someone in the deepest, darkest of waters.

Matt and I limped around Vietnam, unable to engage with the buzz of happiness that consumed those around us. We flew home for the funeral. Our new lives had begun and the irrelevance of favour-choices had never seemed more stark. For the first time in our lives we were truly standing side by side – man and woman, husband and wife, two people fumbling through life together – and we didn't need any of the trimmings to assure ourselves or anyone else of that. I fucking missed my friend and Matt Sellotaped me back together one small piece at a time over the months that followed.

It was around that heartbreakingly confusing time that the swimmers started running free. Mates had started kicking things off in the baby arena before us and the first few baby showers had begun easing into a diary that was formerly the reserve of nights getting mashed up in places called The Purple Turtle.

There wasn't even a discussion, just an accidental moment that turned into a series of them. Everything else in my life had seemed controllable – GCSEs, A-levels, work, even marriage – and then suddenly you're playing Russian roulette with your ovaries centre stage.

We didn't get pregnant for a few months and in that time I started wondering if all the womb-altering contraceptive pills I'd been mainlining over the past decade really were necessary. Getting knocked up is actually quite hard – despite what MTV's enthralling *16 and Pregnant* series indicates.

Matt found the fact he was trying to get a girl knocked up amusing; I was not amused. I wanted a mewling life-form, I wanted our bits to work and I was going to make them work. Looking back, I had gone to the dark side and was quietly starting to get a little sad every time I clapped eyes on a Pampers ad or saw a scan from someone-I-don't-know-but-accepted-their-request-on-Facebook.

My mate George summed it up: 'Just bonk with intent and see what happens.' She now has three children and I believe her advice is solid for anyone embarking on that spunk-fuelled journey. So we carried on shagging to the point where it became a baby-focused fumble and grunt. Every month that unfurled, I'd have fresh hope that we'd hit our target and would soon have a small human who we were responsible for keeping alive. Every month I'd feel that damp signal of disappointment in my undercrackers.

Matt was still revelling in spunking without a condom and actually seeing if the swimmers work. I realised it was going to be an administrative and emotional horror show if we had a kid – I needed to train Matt up and that's where Douglas the flatulent beagle stepped up to the plate.

In those months of bonking with intent, I handed the beagle over to Matt. It wasn't a clear handover; I just stopped doing things for Douglas in the hope Matt would pick up the reins/ lead and see that dogging is hard. He stepped up; he scooped shit off the streets, bathed that little critter and pulled an entire foil-swathed hotdog out of his rectum after a rogue scoffing.

Just as well. I edged out of the bathroom on a grey, insignificant Monday night, clutching the stick of procreational doom/glory. It said three to four weeks pregnant. Matt's response: 'We need to buy a cot.'

The black tears flooded once more. We were ready.

Papa Pukka.

Is your current life pleasant?

Do you generally eat when hungry and sleep when tired?

Are you regularly assaulted, both physically and emotionally?

If the answers run 'kind of', 'yes', 'no', then you're probably in a peaceful state known as childlessness. Congratulations: you are wise and frivolous and free.

But if you're planning on ending that state and delving into a life of parenting, there are some things you should know, which I have summarised in graphic form:

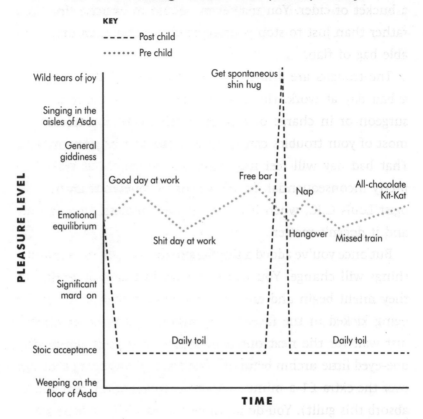

The Post-Breeding Pleasure Well (PBPW) Theory

KEY
---- Post child
...... Pre child

This is the Post-Breeding Pleasure Well (PBPW). It's the development of an idea that was first introduced to me by a former boss who had three children – none of whom have committed major crimes.

The theory of PBPW is simple. Before breeding, our pleasures and woes come as gentle peaks and troughs, and you can mostly introduce the peaks whenever you want. If you like to read, you can spend an evening with your face in a book. If you like to drink, you can spend an evening with your face in a bucket of cider. You may even choose to exercise 'for fun', rather than just to stop yourself from becoming an un-bonkable bag of flab.

The troughs are a little harder to control. But if you have a bad day at work, the chances are – unless you're a heart surgeon or in charge of a large consignment of explosives – most of your troubles can be cured with beer or sleep or cake. That bad day will feel important at the time, but really it's pretty inconsequential. In the words of renowned anthropologist Louis C.K., when it comes to the childless, 'you can die and it doesn't matter'.

But once you've added a tiny version of yourself to humanity, things will change. You will still have bad days at work, but they might begin and end with scooping faecal matter while being kicked in the face. When you miss a train, you don't just wait for the next one, you seethe with guilt about your doe-eyed little urchin being the last to leave day-care (and rage over the extra £1-a-minute late-pickup charge it'll cost you to absorb this guilt). You do all these things with too little sleep. You continue, you adapt, you stumble on.

This is the bottom of the dashed line on the Post-Breeding Pleasure Well: it is deep and wide and it goes on. There are no fun times in the well. No nice snacks. No relaxing Sunday afternoons spent idly farting in front of a televised sporting event. Those lanes of pleasure are closed to you. Fancy a chocolate treat? Best eat it while hiding in the loo so your toddler doesn't get jealous. In desperate need of eight hours' uninterrupted sleep? Pray for an understanding partner and access to a Premier Inn.

But the PBPW is a well because it has high walls – and these sharp, sudden peaks are joys that can be experienced but not explained. They arrive as a spontaneous cuddle, a first unprompted 'I love you', or seeing the wonder in your child's eyes when he or she first sees a real-life duck. Witnessing that moment – the wild ululations, the flapping arms, the drunken-penguin waddle towards something new – grasps you by the belly. It is a quiet peak of unexpected pleasure, like getting a surprise snog from your playground crush. But then your spawn falls flat on its face, bursts into tears, and kicks you in the groin as you try to pick it up. Welcome back to the well: do try and bring snacks next time.

But like an agricultural golfer who manages a single perfect drive in every 120-shot round, or the hapless baker who creates an immaculate soufflé on their eighth attempt, it's those rare peaks that keep you coming back for more. (That and your legal and moral responsibilities: the Child Support Agency is relentless.)

So good luck, champ. The peaks are high and fleeting and the troughs are low and lengthy, much like I imagine them to be with heroin. In fact, parenting and smack addiction have many parallels: they are both financially ruinous, will damage your relationships and leave you with dark, sunken eyes.

But those highs are really very high.

In its most recent figures, the UK's Centre for Economics and Business Research put the average cost of raising a child in Britain up to the age of eighteen as £229,251. In the US, a similar report was conducted by the Department of Agriculture, presumably because children are livestock. It came up with a figure of $245,340 for raising a kid in the US. Neither of these figures includes supporting a child through university or chipping in while they try to earn enough to rent somewhere when they first enter the workforce. If your plan is to go for two children, that's around £500,000 before little Timmy and Tina are off the payroll.

Here are some other things that cost £500,000:

- A five-bedroom chateau in Dordogne.

- A fifty-two-foot, two-berth Sunseeker yacht (nearly new).

- A personal chauffeur (with car), for a decade.

- A Claridge's champagne breakfast every day for the next nineteen years.

None of these things will ever pee on your shirt.

With those basic economics in mind, why do people keep having babies? My own motives were largely selfish:

1. VANITY

Parenting is an exercise in vanity more extravagant than commissioning a portrait or having a bronze cast of yourself erected in the back garden. It is an assumption that there is something so great about you that the world needs more of it. Aged thirty-six, I realised I was not going to become an international sportsman (though I haven't yet ruled out competitive bowls), or have a scientific discovery named after me (unless I become the first person to get a particularly vicious new disease). Nor would I become the next Jimi Hendrix/Thom Yorke/Justin Bieber (delete according to taste). I was content, but I wanted to leave behind more than just a carbon footprint. As the moustache enthusiast and Cuban revolutionary José Martí once said: 'Every man should plant a tree, have a child and write a book. These all live on after us, ensuring a measure of immortality.' All three are much easier than becoming a heroic athlete, Nobel Prize-winning scientist, or revolutionary leader. Though actually *raising* a child looks to be more of a challenge.

2. ELDERLY CARE

I will at some stage die. If I'm lucky I'll be old when that happens, but it's likely to be preceded by a period when I can't feed myself or wipe my own bum. My preference is for some beloved offspring to fulfil that role, rather than an overworked nurse. I realise that's unlikely, but at worst I'd like to think they'll make a six-monthly visit by train/hoverboard to make sure I'm not being left to sleep in my own effluent. Win!

3. THE BIOLOGICAL IMPERATIVE

This is, it's said, something that is within all of us: the urge to breed and continue the species, despite all the evidence about diminishing resources on earth that might suggest we should be breeding less enthusiastically. It's a feeling that says perhaps we might not be complete otherwise: that we won't have done what – in the most basic biological sense – we were born to do. Not everyone hears it, some do and manage to ignore it, but for me it was a right old nag and wouldn't pipe down.

4. ¯_(ツ)_/¯

I really didn't know what else to do. I was thirty-six and needed an excuse to stop going out so much. I'd been a dedicated and enthusiastic social drinker from my mid-teens, and there's only so much of your life that you can fill with work, food and boozing, particularly when hang-overs take longer and longer to edge away. So if not kids, then what? I had no plans to take up golf, and one or two friends had begun to breed and they didn't seem to be regretting it (though at least one went through a period of rapid and hilarious hair loss). But also, it was curiosity. There is little more tedious to the childless than being told what being a parent is like. There is no adequate way to explain the insuppressible, unquestioning love that main-tains you through the many testing times, and any effort to do that immediately becomes preachy or patronising or pompous. So in the end, I decided to find out for myself.

5. ANNA WANTED TO

This, in truth, was the kicker. We'd tried to be cool. We'd said things like, 'I'm not sure we ever need to have kids', and I largely believed them. But when Anna told me that she was ready, then I was too. Kind of.

●

Timing

Last year, the average age for first-time mums in England and Wales was twenty-eight and a half, while dads were thirty-two and a half. It was also the first year that first-time mums aged over thirty-five (21 per cent) outnumbered those under twenty-five (20 per cent). We're having kids later than ever, because we now (mostly) get to choose when we start a family, rather than having one because we have no other option. I have friends my age who started young and will have packed the last one off to university/borstal/earn-their-own-bloody-money by the time they, as parents, are fifty. I have others who haven't yet begun, and some more that don't ever want to. Whether it's a drunken hump and a forgotten pill, or a meticulously sketched life plan with colour-coded spreadsheets, there really is no perfect moment to introduce a small, demanding human into your life. They arrive, you adapt, and all is (mostly) fine.

I bought around two more years of childlessness when we took in an obese beagle called Doug. He had two expressions: maniacal zeal (whenever food was within twenty metres) and pained disappointment (all other times). He once had a minor heroin overdose after scarfing up an addict's leftover tinfoil from an Amsterdam gutter, and had an unfortunate predilection for eating tights, which always led within twenty-four hours to the kind of ribbon tricks not often seen outside the bars of Bangkok. When a couple buy a pet, it's practice for a baby. It's a trial for keeping another thing alive and demands more commitment than a yucca plant.

The shift from canine to kiddy can be a tricky mental adjustment to make and I was slow on the uptake. For years Anna had told me she wasn't that fussed about marriage and I gratefully believed her. I was 99 per cent* sure I'd found my lobster – the snappy pink crustaceans being creatures that mate for life – but my parents had divorced when I was young and I was pretty ambivalent about the institution of marriage, with its cost, faff and funny suits.

At a certain point it became clear that she really was keen. I hatched vague plans (by which I mean, had a fleeting Google for clifftop spots in Greece ideal for proposals), and told myself 'soon', which meant probably a year or so down the line. But I didn't realise the urgency of the situation until, in the middle of an argument, she burst into tears and said, 'Why don't you

---

* Even though 99 per cent is really a lot, it is not always appreciated by your life lobster when you tell her that you're 99 per cent sure she's the one. You can try explaining that, in purely philosophical terms, it's impossible to be 100 per cent certain of any future event, but that just DOES NOT WASH.

want to marry me?' I dropped to one knee on the spot, in the IKEA-drenched kitchen of our tiny apartment in the Amsterdam red-light district, by the open dishwasher I had been huffily filling a few seconds before. She said yes.

The shift from newly-weds to parents-in-waiting came soon after, partly prompted by a tragedy. A few days after we danced and drank with her at our wedding, our friend Toni committed suicide.

When a young life is suddenly lost it tends to focus the minds of those left behind. I think in some way it focused us on starting a family, and Anna in particular. A few weeks after getting back from Vietnam, I was telling Anna how great I thought it would be to 'just enjoy being married for a while'. Her view was different. There were no tears by the dishwasher this time, but a quiet word on the sofa. She told me she was ready and didn't want to wait any longer. And that was enough for me.

There can be few questions more intrusive than 'are you going to have kids?' when you consider the possible answers:

'No, I'm infertile.'
'No, she's infertile.'
'No, we hate children.'
'Yes, just not yet.'
'Maybe, but we keep having miscarriages.'
Or, most troubling of all: 'Yes, we're trying', with the implicit message: I am now spunking freely.

And yet there is something about being recently married or a long-standing couple that makes people think it is absolutely within the realms of reasonable conversation to quiz you on the state of your combined eggs and swimmers. In such situations, I'm reminded of the response of Jimmy Carr: 'We can't have kids . . . the way we do it.'

But eventually, if we decide that we do want children, we must send our soldiers over the top. We must take the gloves off, send the sailors out to sea and bonk for the purpose that bonking was invented for. Or, alternatively, rent a womb, borrow some eggs or break out the turkey baster. Whatever your situation, this can be a strange psychological shift. Sex education in the UK is routinely criticised and historically our teenage birth rates suggest that is with good reason. But even so, from our early teenage years we are told, very clearly, not to get knocked up. By the time Anna and I decided to start a family I had actively been trying to not get girls pregnant for nearly two decades, mostly by failing to have sex with them.

Then, though, comes a mental shift – 'it is okay to do this' – and the waiting. A friend of mine, who we'll call Zapper, decided with his wife to start 'trying' not long after getting married. Sitting in a budgets meeting one day at the large, formal multinational where he worked, his phone kept ringing. Eventually, apologising, he took the call to hear his new wife speaking very firmly: 'I'm at the doctors,' she said. 'He says if we have sex in the next twenty minutes, I'll almost definitely get pregnant.' Zapper made his excuses and covered the seventeen-minute commute in record time. Nine months later, they were parents.

It can take anything from a few days to many months for women to begin ovulating after coming off the pill, and one shot or years of trying to get knocked up. There's a moment at the beginning when you wonder which category you might fall into. Are you nine months away from becoming a dad, or at the beginning of years of yearning and torment?

It's a time of oddly conflicting emotions. I secretly hoped Anna wouldn't get pregnant immediately, so we could save a little more money. But I was also worried that years of giddy boozing and light narcotic dabbling might have taken their toll, and so wanted confirmation as soon as possible that my swimmers still knew how to swim.

I hadn't had much of a relationship with my own dad past the age of about nine, so felt convinced that I would be an incapable father, destined to raise a child with a bucketful of personality disorders, but at the same time I was desperate to hold a tiny, milk-scented version of myself, just to know what that felt like. I was worried about the things I'd have to give up, such as being able to walk outside at three seconds' notice, or spending an afternoon with no greater goal than reading a newspaper or steering Barnet FC to Champions League glory on the latest release of *FIFA*. But I was also eager to set aside some of my human selfishness and try to do something more meaningful.

And then it became time to pee on a stick. The loo flushed, the tap ran, and Anna stepped into the living room of our flat waving the plastic harbinger of joy and/or doom. In those few seconds, I wasn't really sure what news I wanted. We had been together for five years and living with each other for most of those. We'd moved from London to Dubai after only three months together and then to Amsterdam two years after that. We'd bought a flat in the city, and had settled work. There was no reason to delay any longer.

'I'm pregnant,' she said, and I laughed, then pulled her into my arms so she wouldn't see the terror on my face. It took a few seconds to move beyond fear. And then I thought what I believe most men think: 'My spunk works! My penis has a purpose! Well done, sperm!' This was quickly followed by my next thought: 'I very definitely cannot do this, nor should I be allowed to. But it is imperative that at this moment I look like I can.' I looked her in the eyes and said, 'We'll need to buy a cot.'

As the news settled, we'd look at each other, occasionally giggling and making vague (still unfulfilled) promises about eating healthily, organising our finances, and generally being better people. We wondered who we could tell and we stared dumbly into space. We toyed with ridiculous names and booked an appointment with a doctor. I was nervous and those early days made me realise how little I knew. Five minutes online made it clear that Dr Google was not a source of comfort, and that if we spent any longer in that digital whirl of dodgy advice and wild-eyed worry, we might end up confining Anna to bed rest for the following nine months.

Our approach was: 'Humans have been doing this since we

lived in caves. How hard can it be?' We were deliberately flippant in an effort to calm our nerves, but I also had doubts about becoming a parent and how much I wanted it.

I have studiously avoided commitment for most of my adult life. Through my twenties I moved to a different country roughly every two years. I have been freelance for most of my career. I avoid subscriptions, and calendars make me clammy. Parenthood seemed a big commitment, given that I thought return train tickets placed too much expectation on me.

I'd finally made a decision that I thought I could stick to, but I only realised how much I wanted a child when the miscarriages began.

2

Knocked up

Mother Pukka.

I wasn't aware anything had shifted. It was simply a Monday night at 12.06 a.m. when I felt Matt wasn't pulling his marital weight: that he was being a bit rubbish. He asked, 'Where would you like to go for dinner?' that evening when he could have booked the little ramshackle yet homely tapas place in Amsterdam's De Pijp area. Why question, when you can simply act?

I went at him from 12.06 to about 1.47 a.m., questioning why he couldn't do basic tasks like put food on the table without expecting me to provide a recipe or shopping list. Even when I provided a list, the key ingredient was usually missing.

'Matt, did you get the mince?'
'Oh shit, sorry, I forgot.'
[It was on The List and even a rabid dog could tell you it's the key ingredient of spag bol.]

'Okay.'

Subtext: 'It is not okay.'

It was also abundantly clear that he'd made us buy the wrong flat in Amsterdam. My increasingly swollen (not blossoming) form needed a bath, not a shower, to wash away the day's increasing frustrations – a curmudgeonly tram conductor here, a rustling sandwich wrapper there, the school children in high-vis vests blocking up the pavement. I'd suggested, perhaps too meekly at the time of purchase, the need for a bath and was overridden by his belief that this flat would accrue more value over the years, enabling us to lead a life of dreams. I dreamt of lowering my corned-beef-like derrière into a vat of hot water. I wanted horizontal bathing and he had effectively cock-blocked me. The bitterness ran deep.

There was also the nasal hair. It shouldn't be difficult to coif those rogue follicles. I bought him the Nasal Trimmer 3000 in a fit of post-peck rage. (I say 'peck' because a kiss or snog would have sent me over the edge.) Looking back, I should have discussed the purchase instead of leaving it passive-aggressively on the bathroom shelf. But the man had brought it on himself and by thirty-six should have control over his bodily hair. I've ploughed through acres of stubble on my pins, pits and fanny since the age of fifteen – a quick trim of those darkened nasal bat caves wasn't much to ask, really. 'In sickness and in health' should have an additional clause of 'through rough and smooth' tacked into the footnotes.

It wasn't until I went to visit one of my closest friends Sarah (now Mae's godmother) in a tiny rural Wiltshire village that I realised how emotionally feral I'd become. How I was, perhaps, not being a very nice person. The chalkboard menu in the paisley-printed teashop we visited offered a jacket potato with a choice of five fillings. There was an inspirational quote at the bottom of the menu that read: 'When it rains, look for rainbows; when it's dark, look for stars.' I immediately loathed the place. It also smelt of feet and vinegar.

My request for the full spectrum of toppings was met with kindly quizzing: 'Are you sure you want the coleslaw and the chili con carne together on the same plate?' It was like a red flag to a raging maternal bull.

'Yes,' I angrily wobbled, mildly embarrassed at being questioned on my scoffing needs and perhaps an octave too high for this delicate tearoom. 'Yes, I would, if that's okay? With butter, and also salad cream on the salad. But no tomatoes and none of it "on the side".' Do not question my eclectic approach to carbohydrates.

My friend ushered me to a corner, away from the deli counter and quietly prying eyes of the lovely folk who oozed concern over my decimation of the humble jacket potato, and asked if I was okay.

'Like, are you really okay?'

When we flitted around European capitals as university youths, she would sometimes carry an emergency Mars bar in her bag for those moments when I'd go into a dark place.

My *hanger* had been known to drive wedges between us: 'Can we just pick somewhere to eat? A currywurst is a frickin' currywurst.'

I knew I needed to explain myself. 'I'm pregnant,' I said.

Her relief was palpable. I think she'd felt I'd gone rogue when I was trying to book flights to see her. She'd had to miss an important family lunch to meet me.

The fog was lifting and it was starting to become clear that, fuelled by the hormonal cocktail pumping through my system, I'd entered martyr territory – that sense that I was the first person in the world to get up the duff. But I had to piece this emotional jigsaw together myself – anyone else hinting at maternal martyrdom would have come a cropper.

On my return to Amsterdam, reflecting on Spag Bol-gate and defiantly inhaling extortionately priced dry roasted peanuts on the flight, I swore to come out of this self-absorbed fug and start liking Matt again. I looked back ever so gently on some of my recent conversations with him – the majority of them around 12.06 a.m. when he had a 6 a.m. start the next day – and realised it might be tough for him living with someone who doesn't want him around.

His furrowed Celtic brow started gradually softening as I explained my jacket potato revelations and how it had made me realise that pregnancy had overshadowed the sunshine and light he'd initially signed up for. I pledged to be a better human (not the sort who would see 'rainbows in the rain', mind). I stashed the nasal trimmer out of sight and for a fleeting moment all marital harmony was restored. It was perhaps then – at around eight weeks pregnant – that it hit us that we were making a human: that it was the size of a mung bean, and we snogged, not pecked, for the first time in too long.

Sex was horrible mainly because I felt like a blubbery seal being rolled off a rock and prodded with a French baton. But a fumble in the jungle – however uncomfortable and seemingly disappointing for both parties – can cut through the blather like no words can. I wanted him around, after all.

The next week, in the morning, in the evening, at every hour, sickness hit like a vehicle that hadn't had an MOT in seventeen years. I was cycling to work in some maternity pleather leggings when I knew I was going to vomit. I hastily clanged to a halt and managed to aim the chunder towards a flowerpot as the morning commuter traffic stared on in equal measures of amusement and disgust. At nine weeks pregnant I wasn't properly showing, and so the assumption from strangers was no doubt that I was severely hungover from the night before. ('These English girls' was a constant slight from the local, slightly-more-wholesome Dutch community, who seemed to believe that we, as the female contingent of an entire nation, hop on any penis we stumble across, funnel WKD and love sequins.*)

While the pleather leggings didn't help my cause, they were wipe-clean and that was a positive among many negatives. I'm not sure it helped at the time that I worked as a copywriter

* What happened in Northampton's Ritzy stays in Northampton's Ritzy.

for a fashion label – the boldly named SuperTrash (or 'TrashBag', as my dad once innocently referred to it). The average age of the girls who worked there was twenty-six. Out of a staff of sixty-seven, only three had kids. It was all clackety heels, polished marble surfaces, ironic neon signs and waif-like silhouettes. When the midriff-baring cut-off top came into fashion, it was hard for me and my bump/lump to applaud the sea of bronzed abs wafting about the place. Sisterhood was out of the window; the chunder bus had trundled into the building.

It was around eleven weeks that I announced to work that I was knocked up. The Dutch are a brilliantly blunt bunch. While Brits in meetings might say, 'I love your idea, but have you thought about trying this?', the Dutch will go for the jugular with: 'I don't like it, it's not good.' It took a while for me to come round to this refreshing no-nonsense approach, and in the process it made me realise the indirect guff we tend to spout in the UK.

So when news spread among what seemed like a modelling sorority, I became quite the centre of attention. Not only was I the only English girl working there – the only Dutch word I'd learnt was *zwaffelen* (verb: to slap someone or something with your flaccid penis) – but I was also one of the few who had allowed the swimmers to paddle to home base.

'That's so funny,' said one colleague. 'We were wondering why you keep being sick and at the same time are getting so fat!'

To boldly leap towards bizarre eating disorder, instead of potential pregnancy, gives some indication as to where these girls' lives were. I panic-bought another four pairs of pleather leggings and prepared to saddle up for the bumpy, stretch-marked ride. It was already clear aesthetically that I was a grower *and* a shower – no neat basketball bump 'popped' out. At eleven weeks, I resembled the Michelin Man after an all-you-can-eat buffet. Plus I had to share the pregnancy limelight with HRH The Duchess of Cambridge, who looked like she'd had nothing more than a Nando's throughout her pregnancy.

I invested in some studded wedge trainers at the time to give the illusion of height with the joy of style and comfort. As I landed in the slightly more straight-laced Bucks to see my friend Charlotte one weekend, before she even hugged or congratulated me about my impending pregnancy she laughed hysterically at my footwear: 'What the fuck have you got on your feet?'

On reflection, the wedge-studded trainer does little for the pregnant silhouette other than to leave you lurking in Teletubby-meets-Leaning-Tower-of-Pisa territory.

But perhaps the most awkward bit of announcing Project Procreation was around family. My parents and sister knew the day I peed on the stick, but great-grannies and aunties now knew I'd had The Sex. The lump in front of me was like a copulation beacon blurting, 'They've bumped uglies, folks.'

One uncle kept saying nervously, 'When you produce . . .' Like: 'When you produce, will you return to England?' Or, 'When you produce, will your mother fly over?'

Produce. The word made me feel slightly nauseous and unsettled. I knew deep down I wasn't a battery chicken about to lay an egg, but it was hard to see the wood from the hormonal trees at that point.

My sister was no help in allaying any deep-rooted fears of what lay ahead. 'I can't decide if you look like a King Edward or a French Fingerling (*Google it*). Either way, it's definitely a spud. You definitely look like a spud.'

But there was little to bemoan, really. While I wouldn't go as far as 'blessed', we were certainly lucky to have this little nugget nestling in my seemingly hostile uterus.

There's little out there in sexual education on things not working out. I remember from Biology GCSE the plastic uterus with a creepy baby that slots in and out; I remember like it was yesterday Mrs Baines slipping a condom on a banana. But I don't remember anything on miscarriage, polycystic ovaries, endometriosis or the human reproductive bits simply not working. That part came as a surprise when we suffered a number of heartbreaking false starts.

Miscarrying three times was not in our life plan. To be honest it wasn't even on my radar when we ditched the contraceptives and went at it freely.

But having navigated the heartbreaking, mind-altering pain of losing a child – losing a little part of yourself – I felt a primitive need to live as though this one was going to happen. I started to allow my mind to wander to the future and everything that this little flicker of life could mean. I was tired of treading carefully around my emotions; preparing for the sickening moment you find the first spot of blood in your knickers. I was tired of being embarrassed about my bits not working properly. I fought tiredness this time with relentless positivity. In many ways, I channelled Mr Tumble in CBeebies – all coat-hanger smiles and turbo jazz hands with a hint of someone on the edge.

Unlike during the previous futile pregnancies, when I kept it a closely guarded secret for fear of painful conversations ('How far are you now?' . . . 'Oh, er, this one didn't work out.'), I told everyone and anyone who would listen that I was up the duff.

The local organic food shop owner was first to be informed. Even though he didn't speak English, he nodded empathetically as I was gurning and energetically pointing to my belly. Looking back he probably thought I was (a) mad as a box of frogs, (b) about to tap up Slimming World, or (c) on mushrooms from the nearby Mellow Yellow. I'd later learn my second word in Dutch, *zwanger*, which means pregnant. And then maternity leave, *zwangerschapsverlof*. The latter tended to cover folks in a fine saliva spray when I said it, but it was bandied about all the same to show my extensive integration into Dutch culture.

After the organic food shop owner, I told my mate Pippa. She had ridden the miscarriage wave with me and was the person who fixed my skittish mind in those dark, seemingly barren days with a bosomy hug, a builder's brew, a stack of Jaffa Cakes, and a heartfelt 'It's shit; I'm here.' She made me realise empathy was best in those tricky procreation realms, not sympathy. I'd heard enough of 'at least you can get pregnant' from well-meaning aunties. I wanted someone to clamber in the dark hole with me and sit there plaiting my hair as we watched *Keeping Up with the Kardashians*. Pippa was more than just there; she made me godmother to her daughter Immy – just after we'd had our third miscarriage. It was a much-needed light in what seemed like quite a dark, endless reproductive tunnel. If ever there was a moment that defined sisterhood for me, it was that. One woman giving another a role in a child's life – a life that seemed far from my reach at the time.

Third on the line-up was our local ruddy-faced pub landlord, Hendrick. He gave a thumbs-up and continued pulling a pint (for Matt, not me).

At eleven weeks it was perhaps a little too soon to start bagging the priority seat on the tram, but I didn't care. My worst fears of losing this little mung bean manifested themselves in honesty and transparency with the outside world. I stuck that lumpy muffin top out as a badge of maternal honour – whatever the outcome would be this time.

I was going to live as a pregnant woman, I was going to think of names and I was going to look into nursery décor. This one was going to happen. If it didn't, I'd have a stable of people with me this time who would understand I'd lost something; lost a part of myself in many ways.

The last few times we miscarried, I'd isolated myself from those closest to me – like a little vole burrowing into the soil in the hope that spring sunshine would lure me back to the surface. The offset of that was a sad emptiness and an inability to tell those closest to me what had happened. Saying 'I was pregnant and now I'm not' were words I couldn't find the energy to utter. This time I wanted people to know so that they could offer up a bosomy hug when/if I had to utter the words, 'It didn't work out this time.'

This pregnancy was not going to be swept under the carpet. Hendrick would be there this time with a sympathy pint and some *kaasstengels* (deep-fried cheese snacks).

The twelve-week scan was etched in my diary. While I was merrily blurting out to the world that I was bumping along just fine, I'm not entirely sure my mind had caught up with my vocal chords. That scan had meant gloom and doom in the past, so subconsciously I allowed it to remain just another date in the diary. It was in the same emotional realm as 'do tax returns' or 'have boiler checked'.

The day arrived and I'd had a massive bollocking from a client at work for allegedly messing up some copy I'd been working on. In true Dutch style, he'd foghorned: 'This is not good. Do it again.' I was seething because I'd stressed there had been no brief at the beginning and he was generally acting like a bit of a bell-end. He'd also failed The Knob Cheese Test – anyone who needlessly copies your boss into an email gets the humankind thumbs-down from me. The subtext to my response was: sort it out like an adult and stop waving your digital willy around. My mind was consumed and the scan was on par with an inconvenient dentist's appointment.

I was glued to my phone in the waiting room, surrounded by fellow pregnant folk, awaiting more news from work. I was alone because I couldn't face Matt being there to see yet another lifeless embryo sac as we both searched for a hint of good news on the obstetrician's face, only to be delivered the furrowed brow of concern. I wanted to go it alone.

Just as I was called into the scan room, I received another email from Knob Cheese (still copying in my boss) saying that what I'd done was 'OK' but he wanted a call in five minutes to urgently go through the final press release before signing off by 5.30 p.m. at the latest. It was 5.25 p.m.

I apologised to the kindly OB as I frantically penned an email saying that wasn't possible because I was at 'the dentist'. The OB started lathering up my stomach with that strangely chilled lube as I hit the final 'kind regards' (subtext: feck off you twat waffle) and I was stopped in my digital tracks by the butterfly-fluttering sound of a heartbeat. It was more than a flicker of life; it was a time-stopping, breathtaking thud.

I couldn't tell you what happened next. It was somewhere between sobbing with elation and mourning the loss of the other three little people that hadn't made it this far. The OB said, 'It's looking good.' I was a like a woman crazed, dazed and confused.

What sat slumped before that kindly lady was a sodden mass of black-mascara-stained woman clutching a phone like a lifeline, wondering if anything other than that flicker of life actually mattered in the world. I felt the bleat of my phone as the relentless client tried to bulldoze his way through to my conscious. I turned the phone off; I turned the world off.

It was the first time after three false starts that I'd heard an infant heartbeat. It was the first time through all the heartbreak of losing a child that I felt like I might be a mother.

I took a moment and turned my phone back on to ring Matt.

'We have a heartbeat.'

Papa Pukka.

It's important to get one thing clear up front: pregnant women can be really mean.

You may have seen pictures on the internet of the heavily knocked-up looking serene – leaning back, hands on their bump, a quiet look of contentment spread across their smiley faces like a lady Santa Claus after a particularly excellent mince pie. But like most things on the internet, the reality is very different – you will not 'be amazed by what happens next', that local man is not 'earning £112.42 an hour from home' and lesbians don't act like that in real life.

Similarly, pregnant women do not spend much time contentedly leaning back like a lady Santa Claus after a nice mince pie. They are, in fact, irrational, emotional and irate.

One friend of mine, a generally placid and reasonable chap who we'll call Jeremiah, woke one night to find his (usually lovely, equally placid) wife shouting at the back of his head: 'FOR FUCK'S SAKE YOU SELFISH BASTARD, WHY CAN'T YOU BREATHE MORE QUIETLY?'

Another spent the first trimester of his wife's pregnancy sleeping in the baby-to-be's room because his pyjamas 'made a weird rustling noise'.* But they're very happy now.†

Anna and I have been pregnant seven times. The first time was a couple of months into our relationship. It was unplanned and happened because antibiotics can stop the pill from working (who knew?‡). It ended in miscarriage almost before we'd known it had begun.

The second time was about four years later. We'd decided to start 'trying' and I didn't make the connection between that decision and the really mean woman my wife had become. In fact, in those weeks before we knew we were pregnant, there was so much distance between us that I thought we might be splitting up.

In our early days together, one of the things that had convinced me that Anna might be my life lobster was how easily we came to know each other. When she was upset, I generally knew why and had a good idea whether or not it

* I'm not sure why a grown man would wear pyjamas. Maybe GQ made him do it.
† As far as I can tell – they're not divorced or anything.
‡ Everyone, it turns out. But I stand by our defence that antibiotics manufacturers need to put this in MUCH bigger writing on the packets.

was my fault and how it might be fixed (usually by food, sleep, kind words or a quick bunk-up).

But in those early weeks of pregnancy, I thought I'd made a terrible mistake and completely misread the previous five years. The endless optimist, who went spinning around like a ball of relentless sunshine, had become an irrational grump (that was supposed to be *my* thing). She was normally the one to address any friction in how we were, and would never let us go to sleep on an argument. And now she was sullen, telling me everything was 'fine' when it clearly wasn't, and not laughing in the slightest when I suggested that a quick bunk-up might sort things out (weird).

If I forgot to buy the requested 'rose-scented facial cleansing wipes for normal to combination skin' from the supermarket, rather than just roll her eyes or mock my feeble memory (as had become relationship tradition) she would go silent for an hour before eventually wailing that I clearly didn't care about her any more. Failure to make tea or spontaneously light a scented candle as a silent act of love became sure signs that our marriage was a fraud and I'd been stringing her along for all these years. She once cried angry tears because I bought soy milk instead of almond milk, and this naturally meant I didn't respect anything she had to say.

Then the gloom lifted and it became clear that the previous years had not been an elaborate sham, but she was, in fact, up the duff.

The hormone hullabaloo

There is solid science that explains much of this. At four weeks, an embryo is a delicate muddle of cells about the size of a poppy seed. Its formulation causes a surge of hormones to test the most rational spirit. The main culprits are oestrogen and progesterone, a hormonal cocktail that blends about as well as milk and lemonade. Excess oestrogen can cause weight gain, water retention and anxiety. Progesterone burns fat, makes you pee and dulls the senses.

It's like having a Red Bull for breakfast with a light Rohypnol chaser. Or guzzling a triple espresso and a large whisky, but rather than having these after a late dinner and surrounded by exuberant friends, they've been surreptitiously injected into your bloodstream on the bus to work. Honestly love, it's no wonder you're all over the shop.

The most extreme symptoms tend to come in the first twelve weeks, with things typically levelling out by week twenty or so. In most cases, those shifts affect mood, libido, memory, eating habits and sleeping patterns. There will also probably be puking, fatigue and general rattiness.

For the pregnant one, the received wisdom is to understand that you are not going mad, but are being mucked about with by Mother Nature. So you should relax as much as possible and try, every now and then, to think your way to the Zen-like state of a female Santa Claus after a particularly satisfying sherry (though without actually drinking any sherry).

For the partner, the choice is simple: suck it up. Technically, that's not a choice as there's only one option, but it is nice to think that you've chosen to be an understanding person, rather than have it foisted upon you against all your most natural instincts.

You will find yourself in the role of bookmaker's dog: gently padding about the place hoping for some affection, but more often than not receiving a stray boot to the ribs for things that aren't entirely your fault.

You'll be a fetcher and a carrier and a general panderer to needs. Many of these needs will be unreasonable but you'll meet them anyway, because your partner has a constant cocktail of uppers and downers racing through her bloodstream.

Of course, if you too have a constant cocktail of uppers and downers racing through your bloodstream, you might want to re-evaluate things. You're about to become a parent, for example, so it might be time to cut back.

I found myself torn, through most of our pregnancy with Mae, between two primal instincts. The first was an underlying guilt that I wasn't doing enough – that I didn't earn enough, that our apartment wasn't safe, that I didn't provide enough (any) foot massages, and so must remedy these things all at once all day long. I would inwardly congratulate myself for each cup of herbal tea provided or vaguely healthy meal sourced. On the day I bought a cot from IKEA, I thought I was probably the most selfless man to walk the earth since Nelson Mandela. Honestly, I was going on about it for *weeks*.

The second instinct was very different. I felt that once a new life arrived, mine would effectively end, so I had to capture each moment. Every daytime pint was a gift, each social invitation embraced, every moment of idle reading on the loo to be cherished. While Anna was stone-cold sober for nine months, I spent at least seven months hoovering up boozing opportunities like a student with a freshly minted loan. Given that we lived in Amsterdam at the time, these opportunities were many.

The big reveal

The Dutch pride themselves on two things: directness and pragmatism. (Also: water management, trading nous, beer brewing, Golden Age art, entrepreneurialism, language skills and inventing the 4-3-3 formation. They've got lots to be proud of and they're not shy about it, though they are less keen to discuss the 2 Unlimited* *oeuvre*.)

That directness manifests itself in many ways. In work meetings, I would watch in quiet admiration as Dutch colleagues took turns telling each other that their ideas were 'kind of shit', which made a refreshing change from more British variations such as, 'Well that's certainly one option' (translation: 'Pipe down Jones, you mouth-breather').

That directness is particularly apparent around pregnancy, which tends to be announced as soon as the couple themselves know. Whether you shout it from the rooftops or keep schtum as long as possible, there comes a time when you will need to

---

* They're the ones that did, 'No-no, no-no no-no, no-no no-no, no-no, there's no limit.'

tell people that you're smuggling a stowaway, otherwise they might just think you're really unobservant. Reactions to this will vary according to the group you're telling.

1. YOUR PARENTS

Your parents are likely to be delighted, partly because they'll have a tiny human to squeeze and hand back when the bawling begins, but mostly because they know you will finally come to realise what an ungrateful arse you've been over the previous decades. The one uncomfortable element to the parental reveal is the subtext that you are, in fact, 'doing it': that your genitals, which they (hopefully) haven't seen for years, have definitely been put to use.

2. THE CHILDLESS

Among my childless friends, and particularly those I'd known the longest, behind the polite congratulations and smiles, I saw loss in their eyes and silent understanding. It was a look that said, 'Man down. He's done. No more pub fun for you, sunshine.' There was the realisation that with each new baby, the chances of them having to breed increased. Among our oldest buddies, there is something about seeing children appear that clearly declares one thing very loudly: you OLD.

3. THE EAGER DADS

Some were excited – giddy, even – to have someone else to share their agonies with. They were almost too enthusiastic, like guys who'd spent the mortgage money on a pyramid scheme they couldn't get out of, and who would only be solvent again if they convinced seventy-three more people to do the same. They'd say things like, 'It just keeps getting better!' and 'Every new stage is amazing in a different way!' while forcing a sparkle of enthusiasm into their dark, sunken eyes.

4. THE WAR-TORN DADS

Others were quieter, like firm but kindly two-tour sergeants in Vietnam welcoming new recruits. They didn't want to molly-coddle, but also didn't see the need to reveal the full horror before the shooting starts. Because, goddammit, you can't explain hell to a man who's never been there. Picture Willem Dafoe's Sergeant Elias to your Chris in *Platoon*: a firm stare, eyes full of knowledge, and a countenance that says, 'Listen to me and you might just make it out alive.'

5. THE LOW-LEVEL PSYCHOPATH DADS

Then there were the laughers – those who knew what lay ahead for you and revelled in it. The kind of men who would go out in a storm just to show off their umbrella to those getting wet. They'd say things like, 'Whatever you do, stay up top at the birth – it's like watching your favourite pub burn down!' or rush to fill you in on the horrors of sleep deprivation, marital strife, and those funny little tubes for sucking the snot out of infant noses.

How to appear like a dad-to-be

There then comes a time when you have to appear dad-like yourself. This is mostly for the benefit of medical professionals and in-laws.

Several millennia of grunting patriarchy means that society sets parenting expectations low for men (well done LADS!), but this is shifting and it's likely that your baby-mama will want you to do more than spunk at the beginning and dish out the cigars nine months later.

Her body is sucking the life force from her to supply your spawn, her chemical makeup is in open revolution against her sanity and, along with the hope, joy and expectation, she is likely to be feeling more fearful than the last trumpeter on the *Titanic*. So you will need to step up, even if you're all aquiver yourself.

My main tip is a subtle point of syntax: it's not 'she's pregnant', it's 'we're pregnant'. While no one expects you to co-host the foetus, it is a solid linguistic marker of togetherness. As well as reassuring your partner that you're committed to the human-in-waiting, it establishes to the wider world that you are a 'nice man'.*

Again, those years of low expectations work well here for male partners of pregnant women. In the same way that your granddad might have been amazed to hear a woman talk

* Right up until someone points out that YOU personally are not pregnant at all and should stop trying to extract the credit until you can do some actual gestating.

knowledgeably about how to fix a fan belt, society at large tends to be gently charmed if any man who isn't a gynaecologist can say 'perineal massage' without laughing.

But remember, the slightest slip can set things back. At one scan for Mae, I asked the wand-waving obstetrician if she thought there was 'enough womb to manoeuvre'. I'm not sure Anna's ever really forgiven me.

So, there are some basic pieces of process information that it's important to understand.

1. NINE MONTHS IS A LIE

It's forty weeks, start to finish, which is really getting on for ten months. We've been lied to for all these years.

2. SCANS

You tend to get two, though this may increase with high-risk pregnancies. The first, usually around twelve weeks, will give you your due date and you'll usually also have your NT (nuchal translucency) scan. Along with a blood test, this is part of the combined screening for Down's syndrome. This is provided as a number – an XXX to 1 chance. Whatever that figure, it can never be high enough to put your mind truly at rest. At the beginning of the scan they turn on the audio and there is an echoing silence – an absence of sound that feels incredibly loud. There is a screaming emptiness, like distant wind in a cave or a faint transmission across space. Until finally, hopefully: DUH-duh, DUH-duh, DUH-duh. You may find yourself welling up, you may find yourself staring numbly ahead, or you might just be wondering if you'll be done in time for dinner. But for many, this is the first time that it all becomes very real.

The second scan is at around twenty weeks and checks for 'structural anomalies' in the baby, an unfortunate phrasing that makes it sound like a housing surveyor's report. But it's also the first time you will see something that looks really human. The skull is visible, along with the first delicate slope of the nose. You can see legs and arms and ribs, and might even be able to see some fingers and toes. In decades past, this scan would have been an indecipherable blob of shadows and lines. But the clarity of today's scans mean you are likely to get your first clear view of your child. Our twenty-week scan with Mae was a new milestone, and a stage we hadn't reached with the three previous pregnancies. I got a tiny piece of grit in my eye and squeezed Anna's hand.

3. DEVELOPMENT

The tiny person-to-be in your partner's womb goes through some distinct phases, from spermy-eggy mush, to web-fingered critter, to developed-human-living-happily-inside-another-human a bit like a Russian doll. Keeping track of this development is amazing and many apps, websites and books give comparative sizes to help you understand how big your work-in-progress might be. Unfortunately, they usually do this with an array of exotic fruits and vegetables that you may not be familiar with. (I mean, what the chuff's a jicama?) For this reason, I have provided a comparative size chart of my own, here:

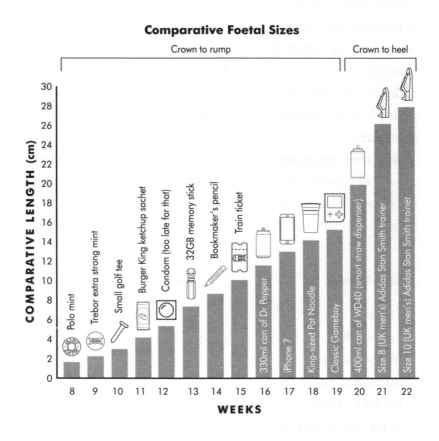

Comparative Foetal Sizes

Now, there is much that can be achieved within forty weeks. You can become a competent blues guitarist. You can circumnavigate the world on foot at a steady jog. You can self-build a home from scratch, including planning applications (which really puts my IKEA struggles into perspective).

It is enough time to prepare all that you might need, but there's also a lot of time when nothing much happens. There is growing and eating and resting, but for most of the forty weeks, the gestation just kind of takes care of itself. While this is good, it does give the mind time to wonder. Will my child be healthy? Will it be a numbers person or a words person? What happens if it gets my fat nose and my partner's giant ears?

And then there are the words that lurk at the back of the expectant parent's mind: disability, stillbirth, miscarriage. These are unspeakable worries, but they do prepare you for the low, lingering concern that you'll feel on most days as a parent.

The basics

There is so much advice. There are thousands of books and guides. But you could probably fit all the really important stuff onto an A4 crib sheet. If you have any questions, speak to your family doctor. If he or she isn't any help, ask to speak to another one. Dr Google is no use to you, as it has been scientifically proven that any online symptom search will result in a diagnosis of death within three clicks.*

* It hasn't, I made that up.

For a quick online nose-about, the pregnancy and baby pages on nhs.co.uk and the various babycentre.com websites all offer clear, reliable information. In the meantime, here are some basics.

PRENATAL DEPRESSION

It's estimated that for around 15 per cent of women, the usual ups and downs of pregnancy develop into something more serious. The Office on Women's Health in the US list signs of prenatal depression as: feeling restless, moody or sad; crying a lot; having no energy; eating or sleeping too little or too much; lack of focus; memory problems; feeling worthless; losing interest in things you used to enjoy; withdrawing from friends and family; aches and pains that don't go away.

Each case is individual, and most mums-to-be will recognise some of the above. If symptoms persist for more than a week or two, you should speak to a doctor.

FOOD

Guidance changes regularly, so keep checking whichever government advice you trust the most. The site nhs.co.uk has an exhaustive list (search for 'foods to avoid in pregnancy') that currently includes: some soft cheeses; partially cooked meats; pâté; liver; some raw fish; unpasteurised dairy; shark, swordfish and marlin;

some cured meats; some game; partially cooked eggs. And the current advice is to avoid alcohol completely.

SUPPLEMENTS

The NHS currently advises against taking high-dose multivitamin supplements, fish liver oil supplements, or any supplements containing Vitamin A. It also recommends taking 400 micrograms (mcg) of folic acid each day and that you might consider taking a Vitamin D supplement.

3

False starts

The bits they don't teach you in sexual education are as follows: positions, orgasms, lubrication, labial overhang, and losing - or struggling to make - a baby. There's so much taught about stopping procreation that you feel a false sense of security that you'll get knocked up the minute your contraceptive admin becomes lacklustre. But that's not always true and when it is, it doesn't always work out. So this chapter is about miscarriage. It is a chapter of our lives - a chapter in one in six women's lives - that was part of the rickety journey to making a small version of ourselves. If you'd prefer to skip it, head straight to Chapter 4 for all the fun of the final trimester.

Mother Pukka.

'The spontaneous expulsion of a foetus from the womb before it is able to survive independently.'

I remember in my first pregnancy Googling the term 'miscarriage' just after I started bleeding and being greeted with these brutal, clinical words. 'Expulsion' – it sounded so detached and finite; like an under-aged youth being chucked out of a booze-laden corner shop.

I didn't find much more solace in the parental forums that generally hosted a slew of emotional fragments or the traumatic story of someone on their seventh miscarriage who had totally lost hope.

No, it was a desolate wasteland of support out there as far as my Googling went. The stats were all in position: one in six pregnancies ends in miscarriage. 'It's more common than you think' seemed to be a phrase ricocheting around the internet.

Social media was brimming with photos of cupcake-rammed baby showers, impeccably filtered post-birth pics and trium-phant videos of toddlers staggering across carefully styled living rooms. And yet I was unable to pass 'go'. I was looking at everyone else driving around on the road and wondering why I'd failed my test again.

Ask every one of the parents behind the lens, however, if they'd had a miscarriage, knew of someone who had, or feared it might happen to them and the resounding answer would be 'yes'. Don't get me wrong, I'm not against cupcakes, filters or bosomy parental hugs, but this polish doesn't always reflect what's gone before. It's about sisterhood – or parenthood, to be specific.

Having mourned three miscarriages before we had our daughter Mae and another two before our daughter Eve, I know what it is to feel like a pariah in the maternal world.

A nappy ad on the Tube once left me sobbing uncontrollably, while friendships with mothers became punctuated with irrational jealousy from my side and an inability to know what to say from theirs. A weekly email from babycentre.com showing the size of my now inviable foetus would leave me numb. It was, undoubtedly, the loneliest period of my life.

The truth is that miscarriage is part of life; it's part of the terrifying, yet brilliant, road to procreation. Katie Price is one of the few celebrities to speak up on the issue after suffering a ten-week miscarriage in 2009.

'It was on the screen and the doctor simply said, "No, it's . . . it's died . . . it's gone,"' she said. 'I was confused . . . I said to him, "But the hCG levels have gone up, so surely that means there is a pregnancy?" And inside I'm thinking, "If I wait, will it form, will a heartbeat come?" All this insanity goes through your head. And obviously it didn't. But I had to accept, it's part of life. It's a part of creating life.'

She admitted something hordes of parents haven't: miscarriage is a part of pregnancy. It happens, it's awful; the rubbishness of a uterus not working is unquestionable. But yes, it's common, and even more Googled than Price herself.

But 'common' doesn't mean sweep all emotion under the carpet and soldier on into the office because you don't want your boss to know you are 'trying'.

Common doesn't need to mean forgetting that little life that might – or might not – have had a name.

Common doesn't mean an absence of grief.

The slew of mothers I know who got knocked up without

a hitch may not have had miscarriages, but they have known fear. The fear of losing a part of them along with their tentative hopes for that little life. The fear that suddenly the 'peanut' or 'bean' they've grown to love and nurture with a holistic cocktail of chia seeds, pregnancy tomes and folic acid tablets might not materialise. The fear of decorating a nursery too soon. The fear that every scan will reveal a quiet emptiness – a silence that pierces even the hardiest souls.

It's certainly not about a fear of over-sharing. The women I know are good at writing, talking, crying and expressing their fears (and when that fails, tidying sock drawers with the kind of frenzied dedication of a famished mosquito) to combat life's injustices. It's more about the difference between empathy and sympathy when speaking to someone who has just gone through the pain of a miscarriage.

Having cried, raked through those forums and mourned five children on the way to having our daughters, all I know is, sympathy starts with 'at least you can get pregnant', whereas empathy puts the kettle on, stacks up the Jaffa Cakes and says, 'It's shit, I'm here.'

And yet I felt undeniably alone throughout those miscarriages; adrift from everyday life. Each toilet visit that revealed more blood in my knickers was a stark reminder of the life inside me that was quietly ebbing away. Matt was brilliantly supportive but there really is no easy way of communicating the echoing emptiness that sits inside when you miscarry. It sadly takes one to know one.

Matt was also faced with his own grief along with the broken fragments of a partner who was distant, irrational and distraught. Everyone in the family has at some point imagined that foetus: as a sibling, nephew, niece, grandchild – a vision of the future that gives you all something huge to lose.

Following each miscarriage, I went for the routine check-up afterwards to make sure all foetal matter had come away. It was clinical, it was purely biological and there was limited room for the emotional. I never forget overhearing a doctor tell a nurse that 'the expulsion process is complete'.

And yet, there was one other common denominator across each loss: guilt. The post-miscarriage questioning is relentless, the frenzied guilt overwhelming. Was it that stress-fuelled moment I ran to catch that train? The glasses of wine I drank before realising I was pregnant? Sometimes it goes to an even darker place that haunts at every gynaecological turn. Was it because I had considered an abortion the first time around – abandoning a life like it was an unwanted chest of drawers, only to be reminded it's not your decision to make?

The first time we got pregnant wasn't a life choice I'd made; it happened. As an excitable youth living a carefree life of abandon in London, I'd accidentally got pregnant at twenty-four in the 'honeymoon period' of mine and Matt's relationship – oxytocin, you intoxicating mistress. Having spent the majority of my life successfully not getting up the duff, this was a traumatic turn of events. We were both reporters on 'esteemed' B2B publications (him, *Human Resources*; me, *Horticulture Week*) at the time and felt this was a massive roadblock on our respective journalistic career paths.

I peed on a stick in a public toilet that had those aluminium bogs and wreaked of urine. It was the sort of strip-lit capsule befitting of a scene in *Trainspotting* – bad things had definitely happened in there and I was just adding to its pile of grim excerpts.

I didn't want a baby. I was going to have an abortion.

It was less straightforward than that, of course. A grey fug descended on our relationship; every touch from Matt was a reminder of the unwanted life inside me. I didn't dare think about it too much for fear of changing my mind – looking back, it was a fear of the unknown fuelling my decision. My only experience of parenthood at twenty-four was seeing those bulging nappies abandoned on top of feminine sanitary bins.

Until peeing on that stick, I'd heard whispers among school-mates of girls in neighbouring schools getting pregnant at seventeen. Those whispers were laced with snarky judgement. I'd seen MTV's *16 and Pregnant* and no one looked particularly happy with the outcome. More than anything, I was young and I had no idea what I wanted from the work vending machine, let alone life.

Until I started bleeding. Seeing that pink, almost rose-hued discharge in the gusset of my pants in the work toilets flicked a maternal switch. It was, perhaps, the first time I realised what it was like to have your feelings overridden by Mother Nature's agenda. It was a primal, protective instinct and suddenly it had become clear that everyone was wrong; that *16 and Pregnant* was edited for dramatic effect. I loved Matt, I loved this part of him and I wanted that life.

In those thirty seconds, I flipped from elation to devastation as it sank in that I could be losing this little bundle of chromosomes that had come together on one booze-fuelled Tuesday night. I didn't want it to be 'expelled' from my womb; I wanted it to grow and play rounders in my parents' garden in the summer holidays.

I called Matt and explained this 180-degree change of heart and the potentially dark scenario that was about to unfurl. I checked my messages and there was a voicemail from the Hammersmith abortion clinic to confirm my appointment for the following Wednesday. It was truly a comedy of terrors.

Matt and I arrived at Charing Cross Hospital within minutes of each other. No words were exchanged but a united clasp of sweaty hands bound us together. We waited for four hours to be seen, pinballing between the coffee machine and toilet – to see if the bleeding was worsening.

The abdominal cramps had started to infiltrate my body (and mind) – it felt like turbo period pain. I couldn't bring myself to tell Matt because articulating the obvious would make it a reality. In that short period of time, I wanted to feel pregnant and that there was a possibility of life flickering away inside me. I wanted to feel for a few more moments that there was a chance of one day popping to the 24/7 corner shop and letting this little tinker choose a packet of Skittles before heading to the park.

What I really wanted to say was 'sorry'. With every fresh pad of blood that I discarded, I felt a new wave of guilt that

I hadn't wanted this. That my decision to 'abort' had led to 'expulsion'. It was without any doubt my fault.

'Miss Anna Whitehouse.'

We followed the nurse into the waiting room and explained the situation. There was no mention of the potential abortion because within an emotion-fuelled five-hour period, Matt and I had graduated from selfish twenty-somethings to potential parents – despite the tiny little embryo sack that was being rejected from my womb. We went into that room united as a mother and father.

We were led to the OB ward by a relentlessly positive African sister, passing heavily pregnant women on the way. It was like running the maternal gauntlet – with every mother and mewling newborn I passed under that stripped corridor lighting, I felt a little bit of my heart break, knowing deep down that wouldn't be us. I felt deeply sick that I'd been so casual in my abandonment of this life. I was in that grey no man's land of 'you can't mourn what you didn't want'.

It was the first time I'd felt that chilled lubricant gel on my slightly bloated stomach. I'd seen women in films have their first scan but it was always with a potential beacon of good news on the horizon. The OB's kindly face started to furrow ever so slightly as she searched for a sign of life in that dark uterus abyss. I was watching her face like a hawk, while Matt held onto my hand with the intensity of someone trying to haul a floundering swimmer onto a boat.

Her face switched towards kindly concern. 'I am afraid it's bad news. It looks like you are miscarrying.'

I wondered how many women that day she had said 'It's a boy!' to. I wondered how many had heard, 'Are you sure you don't want to know the gender?' I wondered how many had heard, 'Everything looks great.' I wondered how I was lying there crying for something I didn't even want in the first place.

I wondered but I didn't talk as I was led to a hospital bed to have a pessary inserted into my uterus to help the 'expulsion process'. I'd known Matt for exactly forty-nine days at this point – less than a work probation period – and yet here we were navigating one of Mother Nature's most cruel throws of the dice. Here we were, having decided to abandon a life, only to be reminded that it wasn't our decision to make.

Our 'inviable foetus' passed a painful seven hours later as Matt lay curled up on a bundle of grey wool blankets on a floor that stank of bleach. The nurse asked if we wanted to see the mass of abandoned cells in one of those murky grey kidney bowls. I couldn't bring myself to look but Matt did and it was the first time I'd seen him cry in our fleeting time together. He turned his back on us and edged towards the brashly lit toilet as I sat there feeling an emptiness that, until this point, I didn't know could exist.

I think that was the point I knew we were in this for the long haul. After forty-nine days. For all the frippery of our wedding day five years later, this was the point that our lives locked together without even a whisper of 'I do' or a hint of crisp white linen. This was the messy, raw point of no return, and through a deeply traumatic, sickening sequence of events, we realised we never wanted to lose a little part of us again. We knew we wanted to grow up and grow old together.

We were going to need all the strength we could muster. This would be the first of five miscarriages we would navigate in our relationship. The first of five little lives we would grieve. The physicality of passing that lifeless embryo sac is something that will remain with me throughout my life. As will the realisation that Mother Nature is the one that calls the shots and that it's not anyone's fault.

And, yet, somehow along the way we would surface with two little girls – Mae and Eve. Two sisters who will hopefully have each other to hold onto in those moments when life doesn't go to plan.

How to help a friend or partner (or yourself) through this

- Contact is important. Be there if possible, but, if not, ring. Texting, email or Facebook can feel less personal. A card helped. There is an incredible company called Don't Buy Her Flowers (www.dontbuyherflowers.com), run by mother-of-two Steph Douglas, that delivers gifts – think giant chocolate buttons, glossy magazines, cashmere socks and COOK vouchers – that require no maintenance but pack a fair punch in the 'it's shit, I'm here' department.

- When words seem impossible, a hug or arm around the shoulders makes a difference.

- When you ask how she is doing, don't forget to ask him how he is. So often miscarriage is seen as a solely female grieving process – he has lost a part of himself too and probably has less of an emotionally connected network to wade through the grief with. 'Fancy a pint?' has its place but so does acknowledging he's lost a child. Tears are a healthy response and should never be discouraged. You need to sit in the dark hole with that person. It's the difference between empathy (the ability to share the feelings of someone) and sympathy (feelings of pity and sorrow for someone's feelings).

- If she talks, listening is enough. If she doesn't, don't fear asking a question. Even the wrong questions are better than ignoring the situation.

- If you are the other half, tell her how you feel about losing the baby. Neither of you should be navigating this alone in silence.

- If you are the partner, ask questions about her experience, how she is really feeling and what she is thinking about.

- If you are the partner, touch is important when words fail. A massage can unite two people in the absence of saying anything.

- Encourage her to be patient and not to impose 'shoulds' on herself – grieving takes time.

- Reassure her she did everything she could and it wasn't

her fault – it helps alleviate guilt. You can't see the wood from the hormonal trees during this time so someone else telling you it wasn't your fault makes a difference.

- Grieving is a physically exhausting process and she will probably need to curl up with Netflix for a few days – or however long it takes. Take whatever steps necessary to give her the space to grieve, cry and physically heal one hour at a time.

- The intensity of grief fluctuates. During less tearful times a change of scenery can work. Simply popping to the shops for the Sunday papers can be enough – it doesn't have to be a visit to the National Portrait Gallery.

- Do something practical such as hanging up the washing or take round a hearty lasagne. Even if she's not ready to speak to someone, that homemade nosh can make someone feel less isolated.

- The only advice that's helpful is to steer clear of forums and head towards more informed sites like tommys.org and miscarriageassociation.org.uk.

Five helpful things to say

- **'I'm so sorry about your miscarriage.'**
These simple words mean a lot, especially if you allow your mate to talk further, or even not to talk, as they wish.

- **'I know how much you wanted that baby.'**
Here you are simply acknowledging that something huge has been lost, and opening a door to talk more.

- **'Can I call you back next week to see how you are doing?'**
Often people are sympathetic at the time, then never mention miscarriage again. You can expect the grief to last for weeks or months, so it is reassuring to show your support is ongoing.

- **'I was wondering how you are feeling about your miscarriage now.'**
It's nice for them to have the opportunity to talk about their miscarriage, even if it is a long time later and after a successful pregnancy as well. Parents do not forget a miscarriage.

- **'I don't really know what to say.'**
The good thing about this is that it is honest. The fact that you are available to listen is what's really important.

If in doubt, say something – anything – and be prepared to listen. Possibly the hardest thing, even harder than hearing an insensitive comment, is when people say nothing at all.

Papa Pukka.

I asked her out with a dubious pun. We were both starting out as journalists, eking out an existence on magazines like *Horticulture Week*, *Practical Caravan* and *Human Resources*. The Pulitzer committee was unaware of us.

We worked in different buildings for the same West London publisher and were both sent on a one-day course on media law. I was late and when I arrived I found six or seven young hacks sitting around a table making awkward conversation. I saw Anna and time stopped. The rest of the room fell away as I saw this girl who seemed to carry her own light source. She had golden curls in a bouncy halo and spoke with a posh-but-playful lilt that left me giddy like a schoolboy. I don't think a girl has had such an effect on me since Penelope Pitstop caused confusing stirrings when I was seven years old.

She had mesmeric blue eyes, a husky voice to deliver her sharp and spontaneous wit, and, if I'm honest, an arse that I haven't been able to take my eyes off since. It is a tuckus for our times, a booty to believe in, a rump of such circular perfection that I'd follow it to the end of the world just to bask in its everlasting glory. It was her heiny that won me over and I'm not ashamed to admit it.

Over the course of the day I engineered every possible opportunity to paint myself in the best light. I dropped in references to pieces I'd written for national newspapers, to travelling adventures as a solo backpacker, and to doing manly labouring jobs. I dropped jokes into the group discussions and when we split off into working teams I made sure I was in hers. I don't think I've made a more concerted effort to be 'charming' before or since.

When lunch came we shared an umbrella to a shabby little boozer to eat limp sandwiches with the rest of the group and by the end of the day I'd decided that I wanted to marry her.

Then I didn't see her again for six months. We were both in relationships, we had no friends in common, we worked in different buildings, I didn't have her number and Facebook was a creepy idea in the mind of a goofy American undergraduate. I drafted and deleted a dozen emails to her work address, and hoped that events might bring us together again. Tragically, they did.

On 7 July 2005, four terrorists detonated devices in central London, murdering 52 people and injuring more than 700. One of those killed was an old university friend of Anna's called Jen Nicholson and in the weeks that followed, Anna and three friends decided to hike to the North Pole to raise money for The London Bombings Relief Fund.

I'd been on the Tube that morning and was ushered towards buses with all those other grumbling commuters who were unaware of what had happened.

I'm slightly ashamed to admit it, but when Anna sent around a group email asking for sponsorship for her hike, I used a heartbreaking tragedy and its altruistic aftermath to ask for a date.

A few weeks before, I'd gone to Norway to write a story

about Royal Marine Reservists on cold-weather training. Painted in the right light it sounded suitably rugged – we were in the Arctic Circle, there were guns and survival techniques. If I left out the bits about the warm press van and three-star hotel I might sound relatively butch. And so I asked her if she fancied a drink to discuss 'ice-breaking drills' ahead of her trip (as in 'breaking the ice'. It wasn't a very good pun).

The pun didn't land and she came ready to discuss polar survival skills, while I came hoping for a snog and a second date. She told me she could only spare an hour – her escape line being that she had to 'put together an IKEA wardrobe'. I didn't get the snog but I did get the second date, then a third, and eventually one morning, after a night of guzzling whisky macs, we woke up together.

By the date after that, I'd been offered a job in Dubai that involved flouncing about the world to research and write travel guides. I said yes and asked Anna to come with me. She agreed. We'd been together about four weeks before deciding to emigrate.

And then, in the weeks between taking the job and moving out, Anna peed on a stick, the cross turned blue and we discovered we had a spanner in the works (or, more precisely, a bun in the oven).

A few days later, the cramping began. She called to tell me she was bleeding. I met her at the gates of the hospital where over the hours and days that followed we simply waited, because there is very little that can be done with a miscarriage that early. We waited to see the on-duty obstetrician. We waited while she performed her examination and gave us the news. We waited for a bed and some food. We waited all night, Anna propped up and dozing in her bed, me lying on the hospital floor, us both trying to cheer each other while everything 'passed'.

Our relationship was ridiculously new and we hadn't properly discussed kids or marriage or any such grown-up things. But seeing someone in pain focuses your feelings. If a casual acquaintance has a hard time at work, you might dutifully listen and offer advice, but the chances are you just want them to sort it out so you can go back to talking about sport/boobs/ the weather. If an old, distant relative becomes ill, it's sad, you send flowers, but it doesn't really have an impact. Seeing Anna in the hospital bed – emotionally frayed, in pain, skin pale – crystallised for me how close we'd become and how I might fall apart if she were no longer around.

●

We spent two years in Dubai. While our jobs and many of the people we met were fun, the appeal of the place itself was a little narrow. So we decided to try a European city on the way back to London. I lobbied for Barcelona, and a life of eating tapas. Anna lobbied for Amsterdam and actually got a job. We settled, married and began to try for a family. Two miscarriages followed, one at eight weeks, one at twelve. These were very different experiences to the first. Now we were trying – and failing – to have a child.

When we first made that choice, we were excited and

nervous. We became pregnant quickly, but after a couple of weeks something felt wrong. There was the cramping and a little blood and memories of before. We went for a scan and there on the screen was the empty sac: a little white ring with nothing inside. The pregnancy was 'inviable'. In the mechanical terminology of medicine, the ovum was 'blighted'. This happens when a fertilised egg implants in the womb but a baby fails to grow.

We found ourselves numb, but consoled ourselves with science. Miscarriage is common: about 17 per cent of known pregnancies end this way. We've had ours, now perhaps next time will bring better luck.

But it didn't and the next time – at twelve weeks – was harder to rationalise. I tried to remain logical: let's just keep trying, it'll happen. I wondered about alternatives, like surrogacy or adoption. But all the while a quiet sadness was settling. My sister had her second child and a few days later we flew in to visit. And in the grimly grey and strip-lit Arrivals at Luton airport, as we went to get our connecting train, we hit a wall. Anna couldn't take a step further, and wept in my arms as others walked by clutching perfumes and spirits and oversized lattes. We went to her parents instead, for kind words and convalescing.

Then came pregnancy number four. We had scans at weeks twelve and twenty, all returning good news. At twenty-four weeks a foetus can, in theory, survive outside the womb in an incubator. Before that stage, if a baby comes prematurely, medical staff will not attempt to save it. With each day that edged by after week twenty-four, our hope began to grow and we finally dared to discuss what we might need: the pram we should get, the cot we might want.

And then the bleeding began. It was a Saturday afternoon and we were at twenty-eight weeks: before the lungs have developed or the eyelids can open. Before eyelashes or finger-nails or hair.

I have a dully set face for difficult times. I try to wash away all signs of emotion and think practically. I called a taxi and our hospital, I packed a bag. I inanely asked Anna to try and relax. We held hands in the back of the cab and a few tears rolled down Anna's cheek. I stared out the window as the car idled in traffic and cyclists sped by.

At the hospital we knew our way and went to wait in the maternity ward. A new mum in a yellow dressing gown padded past, a tiny infant in her arms. We were called in for a scan and waited for the confirmation that all was going wrong again.

The scan process is straightforward. Up hops the pregnant woman onto the examination bed to reveal her bump. The doctor squirts a clear gel across the belly from a tube the size of a ketchup bottle. This might only take a minute or two, but it drags with apprehension. You become aware that you might be a few seconds away from very bad news. Then the doctor rolls the ultrasound across the bump, pushing down in a way that always looks a little too hard. They may want to nudge the bump into a better position, or even ask the pregnant woman to shift her belly side to side to get the foetus into a more camera-friendly pose.

Then there's silence. You're in a dark room with just the soft blue glow of the monitor lighting up your doctor's face. She studies the screen and moves the ultrasound.

And then you wait.

We held hands and peered at the screen. To the untrained eye, those grainy shapes are hard to make out. You hope to understand but nothing connects. There are curves and lines of white and indistinguishable blobs of black and grey. The longer the silence from the doctor, the worse you expect the news to be.

She probed with her ultrasound, and asked Anna to raise her hips. Then she switched on the sound and at once we heard the urgent drumming of a tiny heart.

'She's fine,' said the doctor, and we both exhaled the tears we'd been holding in.

'But she's coming now, so we're going to try and stop that.'

They gave drugs to help Mae's lungs grow, and drugs to stop Anna's contractions. She stayed in hospital for the next ten days while I cobbled together the baby room, just in case. Then Anna came home to rest for the next twelve weeks.

We were to endure two further miscarriages after Mae arrived. Each one brought horrors of its own and the fifth was as hard as the first.

But after the second miscarriage, I knew not to make any plans before 'viability'. I learnt to ignore pregnancy, because it can go away so suddenly: to refuse to buy a cot, or a new set of bottles, to put up the blackout blinds or get the Moses basket – I learnt to do these things late, because I couldn't face having them and not needing them.

As well as eating away at you individually, miscarriage also strains a relationship. I wrote the post below after Anna wrote an article about miscarriage for a newspaper. It included details she hadn't been able to tell me in person and I admired how honest she'd been, so I wanted to get down what I'd been thinking. It's the only piece of this book that has been lifted straight from the Mother Pukka blog, and it's included because I'm not sure how else to say it.

●

A man's guide to miscarriage

Do not say, 'at least we can get pregnant'. Because what you're really saying is, 'I did my bit', even if you don't realise it.

Do not suggest that 'it's kind of like a heavy period' because it happened in the first trimester and the internet told you it was no bigger than a peanut, or a poppy seed, or an avocado pip.

Do not say, 'it'll work next time', because those are empty words and you don't know if they're true, and this isn't the same as trying to start a 2002 Ford Fiesta.

Do not say, 'at least it happened early' when she is curled under your arm on the sofa and you have paused Netflix because she started crying. Because it doesn't matter that it was early, it matters that it was there. No amputee was ever made to feel better by being told they should be grateful for a clean cut.

Do not think that everything is fine because a week has passed and she only took a day off work.

Do not fail to be 'the strong one' when she weeps, weeks later, at coffee spilt on a rug. Or when she stands in the kitchen, and with red eyes demands that you get more involved or give her more space; that you cook more or fuss less; that you talk about it properly or stop talking about it entirely.

Do not be 'the strong one' so much that you forget to tell her what you feel, whatever that might be. It might just be that she needs to see you cry to know that it matters to you too.

Do not rush to change channels whenever an infant appears on screen, like you are protecting a child from a horror film.

Do not say, when you discover that you are pregnant for a third time, that this one will 'hang in there', because this is not a half-time pep talk for a struggling under-9s football team.

Do not fix your features to be blankly supportive whenever she talks to you, because in the end you'll just end up looking like you're talking to an elderly relative.

Do not feel ashamed that you are – on some unspeakable level – a little relieved that you have longer to save money or find a bigger place to live. But do not share that thought, either.

Do not forget about the moments when each pregnancy ended. Like the second time when you were drunkenly singing Christmas carols and all wearing novelty jumpers over at a friend's place and she, very sober, came out of the bathroom and said, 'Can we get a taxi home?' even though it was only 9.30 p.m. And you immediately knew what that meant and became very sober yourself too, but you had to keep your big stupid Christmas grin on so you didn't deflate anyone's evening, and just said, 'Yeah sorry, we're off, Anna's tired' and went home to lie next to each other and wait because you couldn't do it in a hospital again.

Or the fifth time, when she was at day-care picking up your three-year-old daughter and was late because there was a signal failure on the Tube, and she had to ask to use the staff toilets (even though the staff were reminding her that pick-up was strictly 6 p.m. at the latest and it's 'an extra pound a minute after that'), and she went into the cubicle and knew what was happening but still wasn't ready for the sound of the little splash, like a penny falling into a wishing well.

Do not let trying stop you from living.

Do not fail to tell trusted friends.

Do not stop talking.

Be kind to each other.

One in six

One in six known pregnancies ends in miscarriage, with about 75 per cent of those coming in the first trimester.

According to pregnancy research organisation Tommy's, one in five UK women who miscarry have anxiety levels similar to people using psychiatric outpatient services. A third of women in the UK who receive specialist miscarriage aftercare are clinically depressed.

Recent research by Imperial College London suggests that four in ten women who miscarry suffer from post-traumatic stress disorder as a result.

For advice, turn to your doctor or try one of these organisations:

www.tommys.org or www.miscarriageassociation.org.uk.

4

The final countdown

Mother Pukka.

Growing a baby makes you feel like a superhero. A really tired, weak superhero who wants to eat and cry all the time and who can't lift heavy objects. A superhero who feels nauseous a lot of the time and has the power to be really angry at supermarket Tannoy systems.

There is talk of the 'glow', but for me it was more of an acne-riddled slump and an endless hangover. Words used to describe my pregnant shape ranged from 'rotund' (thanks Uncle Les) to 'You're definitely carrying a girl; they make you wider-of-the-hip' (cheers random lady on the 55 bus). My sister continued to chart my progress with root vegetable parallels ('You're definitely a knobbly jacket potato now. The ones with the leathery, slightly soiled exterior').

My diet ranged from fifteen party sausage rolls in one sitting to yearnings for anything junk – ideally on one plate, ingested at one time, embellished with a mound of Tesco Value pickled onions. If broccoli even came into my eyeline, I'd start retching like a cat trying to hurl up a furball. Green was bad, yellow was good.

Matt was a lucky guy. I reminded him daily that he'd put *it* in there. On a simple biological note, it is quite impressive that one fairly non-memorable spunk can lead to all this. But it was my duty as the carrier (or 'Incubator' as my dear friend Mark called me) to offer Matt a running commentary so he didn't miss out on anything.

One trough can be covered in two words: bacterial vaginosis. If I ever find the medical person responsible for naming that cruel vaginal ailment, I will have much to say. For that person hasn't considered a woman having to go into a pharmacy to endure the following exchange:

'Hi, do you have anything for BV?'
'Sorry, BV?'
'Yes, BACTERIAL VAGINOSIS?'
'What are your symptoms?'
'My fanny is on fire and I want to die right now having this conversation.'
*'Here you go.' *Failing to make eye contact**

It has to be a guy who branded this symptom so cruelly. Thrush at least is easier to say – thoughts of a tiny chirping bird mask the grim truth that lurks beneath the labial surface (normally that it's as itchy as a non-hypoallergenic hessian sack down there).

For the second trimester, the internet promised me things like Jennifer Aniston-worthy skin, the energy of a spring lamb and a do-me-against-the-dishwasher sex drive. I think, as anyone who has ever used Google knows, it lies. Like when you pop your headache symptoms in and discover you have about four hours left to live.

The pregnancy acne had started around two weeks in. I stupidly hacked away at a small spot on my face in the hope I'd squeeze it into submission. When does that ever work? It was having none of it. This was like poking the dermatological dragon. What came back from that futile squeeze was full acne rage. It spread to my cheeks, chin and, bizarrely, my left ear lobe – no flesh was left unflushed. I felt like Mother Nature had topped and tailed me with blights – bit of BV down below, a dose of raging acne up top.

'It doesn't look that bad,' Matt said one night when I started crying at this cruel procreation twist. 'It'll go.'

Subtext: 'It doesn't look great. I hope it goes.'

I gave the aesthetic department one last throw of the dice with a €15 spray tan, hoping a St Tropez faux glow would detract from all the stuff. I emerged from The Lady Godiva Beauty Salon in Amsterdam's red-light district resembling an Oompa Loompa, as the owner placated my concerns with, 'It always looks darker on the first day.' I spent the next five days indoors. It was time to let go of the aesthetics and focus on the wriggling amalgam of cells inside me.

Many people won't go through skin Armageddon. I was friends

with a stunning American girl who looked like she'd just had a few too many burgers throughout her pregnancy. Then, one must look to HRH The Duchess of Cambridge – we were due within a week of each other so her glossy mane and delicate silhouette were a constant benchmark for my aesthetic decline. Much like the time when Matt and I found ourselves on the Eurostar with the under-18 Brazilian volleyball team (the bronzed norks were out of this world), there are moments when the sisterhood has its constraints. Do not feel bad if you are a grower *and* a shower among a sea of girls with perfect basketball bumps.

Then at seventeen weeks I started bleeding. There is little that offers a better dose of perspective than the possibility of losing that little life within. It was 6 a.m. on an average Tuesday when I felt the sickeningly familiar warmth between my thighs. The fear of loss in pregnancy is not reserved for those who have had a miscarriage – or the threat of one. It is compounded by those experiences (the memory of passing a lifeless embryo sac still sometimes hits me like a slow-moving pickup truck) but The Fear is with us all.

I remember saying to Matt, 'I'm bleeding, we need to go to hospital.' We didn't utter a word on that taxi journey to the Onze Lieve Vrouwen Gasthuis in Amsterdam East.

History dictated that I was losing this one – that he or she was to become another painful memory and that we'd have to go back to 'trying' only to be left failing. I felt then that I just didn't have it in me physically or mentally to 'try'.

We were whisked straight through reception, past the familiar line-up of pregnant women and gurning couples.

We were classed as 'high risk'. There was even a red mark on my file, which made me feel relieved in a way. It wasn't just my mind going to the dark place, our doctors understood. My uterus was on a special list of errant wombs that can't be trusted to house a baby. I texted my close mate Dita as we were sat there waiting to hear the worst. She cut through the heavy mood with: 'Your fanny really is a twat.'

Having met a number of midwives and OBs now, I feel in awe of their ability to deliver news of life and death seamlessly within the same day; often within the same hour. To have to look a woman in the eye and explain she is losing a child must be one of the toughest jobs on the planet. Then to give the news to a couple who have been through seven rounds of IVF that they've got to first base must deliver immense job satisfaction. It's a role that truly giveth and taketh.

I think the toughest moment for both is when you start reasoning.

'But I've read that sometimes the baby's heartbeat can't be heard?'
'Is there a chance all is okay? Shall we come back tomorrow?'
'Can you check again?'

Then, worse:

'You've made a mistake, I want a second opinion.'

You don't want a second opinion, you want a different opinion, but they rarely make a mistake.

My thoughts turned to the burly woman with kind eyes who sat before us with the screen and lubricant-slathered scanning probe. (Is it a probe? It definitely reaches places the humble willy will never stumble upon.) I felt sad for her that she'd been lumped with me and my hostile uterus. Neither Matt nor I could look at the screen, having seen it many times before as a dark empty vision of silent disappointment.

Thud.

I remember the first thud of that heartbeat and nothing else. The fear manifested itself in a gasp of relief as Matt and I squeezed each other like Mo Farah and his wife post-London Olympics gold-medal triumph. It might not be the full 1,500 metres but we were a third of the way along – still running, despite shoelaces that had become untied along the way.

'She's good, your little girl is okay.'

That was the first moment we knew 'it' was a girl. A little girl that would enter the world a few months later on 21 June 2013 at 8.34 p.m. A little girl that continues to prove to me on a daily basis that she's a fighter and won't let anyone tell her she's not coming to the party.

'Oh gosh, did you want to know the gender? I am so sorry.'

We didn't care what the protocol was. We had a heartbeat. We were having a little girl. We were winning at procreation roulette.

But there we were at seventeen weeks with Mae nestling securely in my uterus and officially back in the 'safe zone' and any concerns of acne and derrière expansion banished to the cupboard of shame.

I don't think you will ever fully sit back in pregnancy and think, 'I've got this.' Unlike GCSEs, where there's every chance you'll fail if you don't revise, there's so little control in pregnancy. Those who like to plan have to readjust their thinking pretty sharpish. You are simply a puppet in one of the most bizarre biological productions there is. It's an amateur-dramatic improv in your local community hall, not an Olivier Award-winning performance at The National.

But one thing is for sure: it is entirely normal to have moments of deep-rooted fear that the baby isn't moving enough or if you feel 'different' somehow and need an emergency scan. The miscarriage support charity Tommy's urges mothers to 'always ask' if there are any looming fears and I would second their sentiment. If in doubt, get checked out – let your instinct override internet research.

Some will glide through; get knocked up the first time the swimmers go free and ride the waves of pregnancy sickness like a surfing pro. Others will hit hurdles that shake the relationship and leave the mind and body in need of strong Sellotape to piece them all together again. But the one common denominator across pregnancy is the fear of having chosen a name too soon.

To ease off the pregnancy jitters, we enlisted some help. Our first experience with a doula (who we'll call Debbie) was intriguing. My friend (the stunning American) suggested it might be a good plan to have some one-on-one sessions with this tie-dye smock-dress-swathed Earth-mother lady who had helped many women through traumatic birthing times.

Her primary role was to unite Matt and me through the process so that we didn't enter this emotionally fraught time on diverging planes.

The session began in our living room, with Matt and me instructed to take deep breaths and think about a positive moment in our pregnancy journey so far. At this point, our beagle Douglas let out a noxious guff that could have knocked an entire football team off its feet.

The air cleared and Matt was asked to make his hand into the shape of a shell and 'cup' my (fully clothed) vagina as I breathed deeply. I think in all the antenatal sessions we went to, this moment helped the most in getting us back on track. Alas, it was nothing to do with the 'cupping' or Zen-like breathing; it was down to our inability to stifle the giggles.

There was Matt in our lounge, cupping my fanny as the doula looked on and the beagle guffed away. We both exploded into laughter; the sort of nervous laughter reserved for E-number-fuelled primary school children clapping eyes on a rutting pair of zebras at the zoo. The doula remained eerily quiet and said this was a 'normal reaction' to such intimate, non-sexual touching. We apologised to Debbie and suggested we moved on.

That night we had sex for the first time in two weeks. A little laughter can go a long way. (Our go-to game in moments of distress is 'What animal combinations would win in a naval fight?' Mine is currently unbeaten – The Sharsp. It's a shark's head with a wasp's sting. Bites like a shark, stings like a bee. Matt came up with a Babuna – a baboon combined with a tuna fish.)

We went to one group antenatal session and decided not to have the doula at the birth, but we will be forever grateful that she inadvertently helped us bump uglies at a time when we needed more touch and fewer words.

It was also around this time that we heard about the concept of 'the babymoon', a pre-birth holiday for parents-to-be. It sounded great and we wanted in. One last chance to pretend we were burden-less youths who can simply walk out of the door without a battle to get shoes on a wriggling sprog. We booked a week in the Maldives and bankrupted ourselves for the privilege with credit cards maxed and over-draft overdrawn. Why do knocked-up folk try and do EVERYTHING they haven't done in life in those weeks before splashdown? It was like we were galloping towards the end of the world and we had to rake through the bucket list.

I am less mean in the sun, so Matt was happy and I got to eat everything I wanted without any sense of remorse. I couldn't honestly have told you where the baby started and the food ended after a week and a half of hoovering up everything in sight and slumping on a sun chair reading 1980s Mills & Boon grot. We had one week of absolute unadulterated joy while my mum was fearing the worst – mainly that we wouldn't make it to the hospital, which was a two-hour boat ride away – at home and awaiting our return. A mother's work is truly never done.

The return to the Amsterdam homestead offered a stark contrast of deadlines and dreariness. I was one month off maternity leave, so unable to take my foot entirely off the pedal, while Matt was suddenly realising we lived in a flat that was fundamentally baby-unfriendly. We were not ready.

The first weekend after returning from the 'moon, we went out to a new meatball gaff in town. It was aptly called Meatball and we went with some friends who already had kids and were giving us all the good stuff (the lies) of 'It's such an amazing time. It will bring you both so much closer together. It makes you realise there is something more important than yourself in the world.' We lapped it up like a basset hound unaware that it's about to be run over by a JCB digger.

That night, the WhatsApp messages started flurrying in.

'Anyone else feeling dodgy?'
'I've started throwing up and I'm feeling horrific.'
'It has to be the meatballs.'
'We're down, I've got the shits.'

My stomach started churning and then, boy, did the food poisoning hit.

For hours I cradled the toilet bowl like my life depended on it.

We were twenty-eight weeks at this point – far gone enough for the hospitals to try and keep our life project alive if it slipped out early, but not far enough for the little critter to breathe by itself. I knew this because my dehydrated body started contracting. I went to my reflex of Googling.

Google told me the hospital had to save this one – below twenty-four weeks and you're on your own with no neonatal support to keep the baby alive. It's a fairly brutal line between life and death. I was rushed in once again to that familiar salmon-pink ward. The nurse confirmed our worst fears, that I'd gone into early labour and I needed to be rushed to the premature baby unit at another hospital.

After an ambulance dash across town, with Matt's furrowed brow deepening at every contraction, I was popped into a delivery suite and pumped full of steroids to give the baby a chance to breathe on arrival. I was also given a number of injections to try and stop the contractions and keep the bun firmly ensconced in the oven.

We just had to wait. Once again, Matt kipped on a floor that reeked of bleach. Once again we lay there in solidarity together, willing this one to stay put and give herself a fighting chance. We had a name. Mae was a person in our minds and seeing all the other little people in incubators on the premature floor was a real reminder that our little human hadn't properly formed yet.

We made it through the night with the contractions ebbing and flowing. The rogue meatball had well and truly exited and I'd started to feel a little more in control of my body. By the evening, the contractions had stopped completely and we were told that Mae, our little human, had decided to stay put and the drugs coursing through my veins had worked. Science is an incredible thing.

I was, however, a ticking bomb that could blow at any time and was kept on hospital bed rest for two weeks and signed off work for the rest of my pregnancy. There was a woman beside me who had to remain there for three months after her waters had broken too early. Her exact words to me were 'shit could be worse, *poppetje* [the Dutch for "doll"]' and I kept that close to home during the rest of our journey. She went on to have a healthy baby boy at thirty-seven weeks. Mae was in breech position and unmovable, and given our history we were advised to have a C-section. It was booked for 21 June.

●

The C-section. The abdominal war wound. Anyone who says having a C-section is the easy way out is misguided. Is anything that requires a scalpel and a green screen to save your eyes from the surgical horror show ever going to be a pleasant experience?

I simply wanted to know where and when my baby was going to arrive after years of not making it to the finish line. We'd been told that for us it would be safer and, to be honest, at that point on the road to procreation I'd have delivered the baby from a hot air balloon as Jerry Springer and his merry audience watched on if it meant a safe arrival.

So we had a date and I wasn't going to let Mae arrive at the party too soon. I didn't move for the remaining ten weeks. Well, until Matt twisted his ankle playing a grown-up game of 'it' (touch rugby or 'touch me don't touch me', as my mate George refers to this glorified man tag) and I had to walk the dog and get him ice packs. But other than tending to his self-inflicted cankle, I incubated that little sprog. The finish line was on the horizon and, despite Matt's inability to walk, we were going to get there.

Basic stuff you need to keep a small human alive once they arrive.

Boobs (if they work).

Bottle (if the above aren't playing ball).

Netflix series you haven't watched (for feeds).

Some kind of baby receptacle.

Breast pads to save you resembling a fembot when the mammaries start leaking.

A couple of onesies.

Changing mat – ideally wipeable in case of splashback.

An understanding that you will be tired and ratty.

An understanding that this is normal.

Papa Pukka.

By the third trimester you are well and truly in the pudding club. It will be obvious to all that you are soon to hear the wail of tiny lungs. Strangers will attempt to lay hands on your bump and think it reasonable to say things like: 'Ooh, aren't you big?' or, 'Must be due soon!' or, 'Chuffing heck, love, have you got the buggy in there too?'

Movement becomes more cumbersome and more is required of the partner. With spectacular comic timing, in the latter stages of our pregnancy with Mae, I tore the ligaments in my left leg while doing sport* and was reduced to hobbling around with a support boot and crutches while my heavily pregnant wife went to fetch all the things we needed (and carried them up two flights of stairs to our flat). I maintain that it helped keep her mind occupied, but I do find it best not to remind her of it.

This stage brings a strange mix of physical woes and Pregnant Lady Superpowers (that may not be the correct medical term). Not everyone will experience all of these, but I have gathered them in this chart for ease of reference.

* Touch rugby, to be specific, which is like normal rugby but with fewer people and no tackling. Not a group of grown men playing 'it' while holding a ball, as sometimes suggested by Anna.

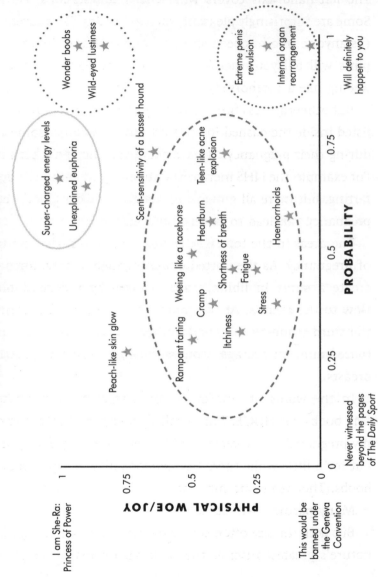

Physical Manifestations of Pregnancy

The left-hand axis covers what the manifestations feel like. Some are surprisingly pleasant, such as 'weeing like a racehorse' (as anyone who has been stuck on a toilet-less train after four pints will tell you, there's an oddly pleasurable sensation to weeing like a racehorse*).

But others are less fun. According to the NHS, the symptoms listed inside the dashed lines affect most women at some time during their pregnancy. (I have adapted some of the phrasing. For example, the NHS mentions flatulence rather than rampant farting, but we're all grown-ups here so let's cut to the chase: pregnancy can lead to violent bum guffs.)

The areas in the top right expose common highs and lows of pregnancy. As the dotted circle highlights, pregnancy can create a surge in libido, partly caused by increased blood flow to the clitoris. At the same time, the pregnant form in the third trimester is hyper-feminine. The curves are accentuated and, on average, women gain two cup sizes on their breasts.

In the words of Lindsey R, commenter on theberry.com: 'My boobs got HUGE. I'm usually a B cup, and by the end of my pregnancy I was wearing a D. They eventually disappeared, but for a little while there I understood all the hype about big boobs. They really are magical.'

Many partners will agree.

But with the size often comes tenderness and this is perhaps nature's greatest ruse: as they approach spherical perfection,

---

* Requires leaving train and finding toilet.

access becomes sporadic. But then beauty is ephemeral, which is why we cherish it so much.

And let's be clear about the other dotted circle to the bottom right: the hormonal and physical shifts that happen during pregnancy can also cause libido to nosedive and any physical contact to become repellent. One friend, a doting father of two who we'll call Ezekiel, confessed to me that for the full term of both pregnancies his usually equally doting wife couldn't bear him. 'I put my arm on her shoulder once while she slept,' he dolefully told me after a couple of beers, 'and she actually hissed at me.'

She also had a heightened sense of smell and told him that the 'stink of him' made her 'want to chunder'.

(As a side note: it's been suggested that this scent sensitivity is one cause of morning sickness. Women who suffer from anosmia – a loss of sense of smell – tend to suffer much less.)

But perhaps the worst aspect – a cruel and unusual punishment that would defy international law – is that the tiny human growing within is quietly rearranging its host's internal organs. The lungs rise, the intestines are nudged aside and the bladder gets squashed. Imagine the bench seating on a London Underground carriage where commuters take up every seat. Now picture a very fat man forcing himself into the middle seat so that the other commuters get squeezed up to the sides, their faces pressed against the glass partitions that always have hair grease on them. In this analogy, the fat man is the foetus, the commuters are the internal organs, and the bench seating is the torso. This unpleasant experience is, unfortunately, a certainty, as shown by its position on the horizontal axis. It is worth clarifying that no scientific research or peer review has contributed to this, but when has that ever stopped anyone writing about parenting? (For a more 'sciency' take, have a look at the Chicago Museum of Science and Industry animation, *Making Room for Baby*.)

Perhaps the best bits of the whole process are those inside the solid grey oval. These are the Pregnant Lady Superpowers. All those nutrients and hormones are there to do good. They are helping life to grow, and there can be some euphoric side effects. Oestrogen and progesterone, while being a calamitous cocktail in some ways, can also create sudden and giddy feelings of joy. They provide energy surges and feelings of wellbeing: the kind of sensations you usually have to buy in tablet form from shady men in bomber jackets. But these are a gift from nature and come without the risk of accidentally ingesting horse tranquilliser.

One research project at the Hadassah Medical School in Jerusalem suggested that pregnancy could even help your body to rejuvenate.

By studying the effects of liver transplants on mice, they found that in young non-pregnant mice, 82 per cent of the liver regenerated after two days. In old non-pregnant mice, only 46 per cent had regenerated in that time.

But in *older* pregnant mice, around 96 per cent of the liver had regenerated after two days: the elderly, knocked-up cheese enthusiasts had healed more quickly than the non-pregnant rodents both young and old. The research concluded that pregnancy hormones could be regenerative.

Obviously, one factor to consider here is that people are not mice. For example, almost 100 per cent of mice have tails and very few humans do.

But much like the parenting process itself, it's safe to say that pregnancy comes with highs and lows. To paraphrase the people's poet laureate, Ronan Keating: '*Making* life is a roller-coaster, just gotta ride it.'

The point of the partner

And so to the partner. At the University of London in 2007, Dr Arthur Brennan conducted a study with 282 expectant fathers aged from nineteen to fifty-five.

They were monitored throughout their partners' pregnancies and found to suffer cramps, back pain, mood swings, food cravings, morning sickness, extreme tiredness, depression and irritability. Some even developed swollen bellies. I too suffered from all of these, but put it down to being in my thirties, having a shabby diet and generally being a grumpy arse. But Brennan's experiment also included a control group of 281 men whose partners were not pregnant, and they experienced none of the symptoms.

One of the participants in the first group said: 'I was constantly hungry and had an unstoppable craving for chicken kormas and poppadoms – even in the early hours of the morning,' which sounds delicious to me, but also like an excuse for being a fat bastard.

These sympathy symptoms from fathers-to-be form a condition known as Couvade syndrome. According to Brennan, 'some people may perceive this as men trying to get in on the act but far from being attention-seeking, these symptoms are involuntary'. He goes on to say that, 'often the men haven't got a clue about what's happening to them', which is something I think we can all recognise.

During our pregnancy with urchin number two, I found myself sluggish and easily tired. I developed a weird limp that I put down to old sports injuries playing up. Anna described this as Being Forty syndrome, and the arrival of Eve has not eased the symptoms.

And while that empathy is nice, it's probably best not to overindulge. If an expectant dad gets to the stage where he's doing pelvic floor exercises he's probably gone too far.

I spent most of our pregnancies unsure exactly what I should do and tended to tackle these feelings of uselessness by making tea. While tea is also nice, it is not always the answer. Sometimes you have to do more, and at the very least pretend to be capable at DIY.

The DIY element in childbirth is taught through antenatal classes. Much as with watching a YouTube tutorial before putting up shelves, you may feel this extra layer of explanation is unnecessary. It's tempting to think, 'This is something that many have done before without too much bother: just drill holes, fix brackets and pop the shelf on top.' Or, in the case of pregnancy: baby is in position A and will leave via exit B or C.

Both are, alas, more complex. Do you know what fixings go with which screws? How do you check for wiring behind the plaster? When is it appropriate to begin perineal massage? These are things you don't want to get wrong.

The pregnancy equivalent of the YouTube tutorial is the antenatal class. It lasts much longer, but isn't interrupted by pop-up ads and is unlikely to lead you down a melancholic wormhole of music videos from when you were a teenager. (And if you are actually a teenager and a parent-to-be, while society may judge you unfairly and you might eventually grow to resent your own offspring for the tragedy of your lost youth, rest assured that getting in and out of a ball pit is much easier at seventeen than at thirty-seven.)

Antenatal classes take many forms and follow several philosophies but the core purpose is to prepare you for childbirth and the immediate aftermath. National Childbirth Trust (NCT) courses tend to be most common in the UK, and involve sitting on the floor while discussing internal organs with strangers.

While NCT is a safe, supportive space for parents-to-be to learn about what lies ahead, it's also a great opportunity to see who else you might have ended up breeding with if things had been different. Take a good look around the room to reassure yourself that you've made the right choice.

Much like hostages in a bank robbery gone wrong, you may find you look upon your fellow captives with a mix of camaraderie and competition. On the one hand, you care much more about yourself than anyone else: if only two people are going to get out of this alive, you want it to be you and your partner. But on the other hand, somewhere deep down, you have a lingering belief in the human spirit, in teamwork and mutual support, and that if you all just work together you can overpower the gunman. In this analogy the gunman is childbirth, which is where it falls down a bit.

One small study by doctors at the US National Center for Biotechnology Information found that, beyond the practical advice offered, antenatal classes can 'support women's mental health because the women give and gain reassurance that their babies are developing normally'. It's pot luck who is in your group, of course, but friendships developed in NCT often run beyond the end of the classes. As one study participant said, 'I think if I hadn't had them, I would have needed something else to keep me sane.'

Our own experience was in the Netherlands, where things are done a little differently, as I discovered when a firm-fingered woman accidentally tickled my testicles. She was a doula – someone who offers support to parents-to-be and attends the birth, but doesn't have the medical qualifications of a midwife. Her approach was very natural and relaxed and she was a big advocate of home births as the best way for a woman to feel calm and comfortable (30 per cent of births in the Netherlands occur at home, compared to 3 per cent in the UK).

'Debbie' was in her mid-forties and so assured in the natural wonder of childbirth that her twelve-year-old son was at the birth of her third nipper and tasked with 'the net' and the role of fishing out poos from the birthing pool.

She had already paid us a home visit, which involved her and Anna straddling each other on our living room rug in the lotus-flower position, while silently holding her hands in areas of great intimacy. Having shown me what was required, she asked me to take her place and watched as I indelicately wove myself in, like a Twister novice after an evening of spiked eggnog. This was to demonstrate massage techniques through the contractions, and how a little rubbing could prove a great comfort.

She emphasised the point at our group session, with about a dozen other couples. The men were asked to stand in the middle, with their partners behind them.

We menfolk were made to lean forward and touch our toes while the doula talked through the early stages of pregnancy. After a couple of minutes, this became uncomfortable. But, being men, we saw this as a competition and persevered.

'It's starting to hurt, isn't it?' said the doula.

We cleared our throats and mumbled variations of 'Oh no, fine actually.'

She then squatted behind me and began rubbing her hands up and down my legs, asking the other women to do the same for their partners. I was her demonstration doll.

'That feels nice, doesn't it,' she said, as her warm hands eased my aching limbs.

She stopped and asked the other partners to do the same. 'Now, what if I went outside to smoke a cigarette, or played with my mobile phone?'

The menfolk made understanding noises: quiet, individual 'mm-hmms' that roughly translated as, 'I see, thanks for the demo; can we stop now, because my legs hurt?'

'Now extra hard!' she said, running her hands up and down

my quads with renewed vigour, until she overshot and slammed four sharpened nails into my own area of great sensitivity. I made a noise like a turkey in a Bernard Manning factory and we didn't return again.

In summary though: most antenatal classes are great, and worth a few evenings of your time.

Be prepared

As you approach splashdown, there are certain preparations to make. One simple but practical step is to ready The Bag sometime around week thirty-two. The Bag will contain all the kit that you and your partner will need for a (hopefully short) stay in hospital.

This is mundane but important and I found that it helps if you imagine you are a member of the British secret service preparing for a mission, or a sophisticated gentleman bank robber who will empty some safety deposit boxes and be out of the country before anyone knows a crime has been committed. Don't go so far as to pack a sniper's rifle or crowbar, however: that would be too much and almost certainly raise an alarm with social services. Here's what you might want to take:

THINGS IN THE BAG FOR THE MUM-TO-BE:
Birth plan, medical notes, two sets of comfy clothes for the birth, snacks and water, any toiletries and make-up, comfy night- and daywear for after the birth, nursing bra and breast pads, maternity pads, phone and charger. Maybe an iPad, headphones and magazines.

THINGS TO INCLUDE FOR THE PERSON-TO-BE:
A rear-facing car seat, muslins, three sets of bodysuits and vests, socks, hat and scratch mittens, a blanket. Some hospitals also expect you to bring changing gear and nappies.

THINGS FOR THE PARTNER:
A button-up shirt, so you can put your newborn on your naked chest (early skin-on-skin contact can help bonding). A change of clothes, a camera, something to read, some snacks. To complete the scene, stick in some leftover travel money and your passport and you'll soon feel like a high-level Mafioso or government whistle-blower, ready to flee for a new life* the moment you get a tip-off that the Feds are on their way. Oh, and pack wet wipes.

And then . . .

Well, you know what's next. It's that bit from the romcoms and the sitcoms. The bit with the tears, fears and blood-smeared medical staff. You two put it in there; now you're going to have to get it out. Yikes.

Prepping the nest

In the UK, new parents spend an average of £1,000 preparing for a baby, according to research by newspaper the *Guardian*. One in twenty spend more than

---

* Do not actually flee.

£3,000. But you don't need quite as much as you think.

In Finland, new parents are given a 'baby box' with all the essentials. It includes a mattress and the baby sleeps in the box for the first few weeks. This little cradle of kit is considered partly responsible for reducing infant mortality rates from 65 per 1,000 children in 1938 to 3 deaths per 1,000 in 2013. The theory is that it meant families had all the essentials to keep the wee bairn warm and safely stored (though many other things also contributed to bringing down those rates over that time). This is what it typically contains:

- A mattress, mattress cover, undersheet, duvet cover, blanket, sleeping bag/quilt.

- Snowsuit, hat, insulated mittens and booties (you could skip this for a summer birth).

- Light hooded suit and knitted overalls.

- Socks and mittens, knitted hat and balaclava.

- Bodysuits, romper suits and leggings.

- Hooded bath towel, nail scissors, hairbrush, toothbrush, bath thermometer, nappy cream, washcloth.

- Cloth nappy set and muslin squares (perhaps switch the cloth nappies for disposables . . .).

- Picture book and teething toy.

- Bra pads and condoms (wise).

Then it's just the bigger items: a cot, rear-facing car seat (even if you don't have a car), breast pumps, bottles and formula, an electric fan (one 2008 study suggested this might lower the risk of sudden infant death syndrome as it helps disperse carbon dioxide in the room), a buggy/pram and a Moses basket – though my sister skipped that and put a blanket and mattress in a cardboard box for her second child. My dad, born in a tenement in 1950s Aberdeen, spent his first few weeks in a cutlery drawer (they removed the cutlery, and even took the drawer out of the cabinet after a while) and he suffered no ill effects (the alcoholism would have probably happened anyway).

The Money Advice Service puts the cost of raising a nipper at £4,000 for the first year and has a decent baby costs calculator at moneyadviceservice.org.uk.

5

Splashdown

Mother Pukka.

Birth: The emergence of a baby or other young from the body of its mother; the start of life as a physically separate being.

You don't need to have had a kid to feel that 'emergence' is an understatement. 'Life-altering, bodily-fluid-smattering, vagina-battering emergence', perhaps? But, then, I'm no gate-keeper of the *Oxford English Dictionary*.

At thirty-nine weeks pregnant I had gone off the spud charts – even my sister was unable to find a root vegetable on a par with my rotund physique.

'An aubergine that won one of those "oversized veg" competitions?' she suggested.

It's like having a bad haircut. The minute everyone in the salon is saying, 'Wow it looks great; you look great', you know that you resemble Rod Stewart and they just want you to cough up and leave without crying. Here's the full gamut of comments that you might receive in the final trimester:

'Don't you look well?'
Subtext: *You are massive.*

'You look ready to pop!' (When you are nineteen weeks.)
Subtext: *You are making pregnancy look scary to me.*

'When are *they* due?' (You are not expecting twins.)
Subtext: *You fat.*

''Ey up, fatty!'
Text: *You fat.*

I was at the stage where words like 'perineal massage' and 'rectal pressure' were being bandied about more often than basic nouns like 'bread' or 'milk'. We were up for a medical elective C-section – or 'through the sunroof' as Matt referred to it – because Mae was in breach position. I wasn't sure how I felt either way at that stage. I didn't harbour any great maternal desires to have a human 'emerge' from my vagina. (Perhaps I was relieved, although I know a troupe of mates who felt very strongly about going through vaginal birth.) But then, having your abdomen opened up like a tin can didn't exactly float my boat either.

I did want it out, though. That's the one thing that unites us all in birth – it has to come out. I had friends who went through a Zen-like drugless experience enhanced by the sound of gentle panpipes, while others had a forty-eight-hour horror show of shitting, screaming, drug-imbibing and pleading before succumbing to being wheeled into theatre for a C-section. There was neither rhyme nor reason to either outcome – the former was my mate who loved a battered Mars bar and considered downward dog a sexual, not yogic, position. The latter was a mate who'd lived a life of homemade crunchy organic granola and had never knowingly trodden on an ant for fear of the karmic backlash.

If you listen to the actress Carol Burnett, 'giving birth is like taking your lower lip and forcing it over your head'. Quips like that didn't help endear me to the natural route but then neither did this about C-section from one of those mildly irksome e-cards on the internet: 'So having a C-section is the easy way out? Is using a chainsaw an easy way to get out of a car?'

But everyone loves to tell their own tale and if you dare Google 'birth story' it's like the internet version of *War and Peace* out there.

It's uterine swings and cervical roundabouts really and my only strong feeling on the matter is that no one should feel guilted or pressured into anything they don't fancy. It's going to nip a bit, however that small human comes out, and as long as the pair of you cross the procreation finish line, it's all good.

The only exception to the rule is my mate Fi, who seems to fart and they pop out. She proudly puts it down to her 'bucket-like' vagina that can also accommodate a wine bottle. (With the cork in – one doesn't want to create a vacuum.)

Scheduling our C-section was like booking in for a hair appointment: 'Would you like 10.45 a.m. on the 19th of June or 9 a.m. on the 21st of June?' It was the difference between a Gemini and a Cancer baby. I'm not massively into star signs unless I'm in a doctor's waiting room and happen to chance upon a copy of *Take a Break*, but my kid might be more astrologically minded than me, so I weighed up the options and realised that my sister was a Gemini and could be a tad annoying at times. Cancer it was.

I proudly wrote 'have baby' in my diary and packed a few things into a bag.

Along with all the baby stuff, there were some knickers, twenty Crunchy Nut breakfast bars – in case the world ended – and a game of *Star Wars*-themed Top Trumps for staving off any boredom.

The contents were not too dissimilar to those required for Brownie Camp in 1989.

I also went for a manicure and pedicure in a bid to perk up the swollen spades and trotters.

Both had to have their polish removed twenty-four-hours later once I set foot in medical realms and was asked, somewhat huffily, by the nurse: 'Did you get the pre-surgery checklist?'

D-day arrived and it genuinely felt like Christmas morning. There was that palpable excitement usually reserved for a present-bulging tree. This would otherwise be a day when I'd go to work and have a cheese-and-pickle sandwich, perhaps, for lunch. Then I'd come home and possibly have a spag bol before hitting the sack.

BUT INSTEAD, A BABY WOULD BE COMING OUT OF MY BODY.

Whether your waters break, you are induced, or are being prepped for the sunroof exit, there is nothing quite like that heady cocktail of extreme excitement and innate fear of what's to come. I felt like one of those skittish racehorses before the Grand National. I knew I had it in me to get to that final furlong but it felt like there were so many hurdles still to pass before that winning post and a hearty nosebag.

The ratio of excitement to debilitating fear was, however, strongly skewed to the former. We'd waited three years and endured our fair share of heartache to get to this point and I was going to cash in those moments of relative joy.

Food was the only thing that caused me real gip at this point. I'd been told not to touch a scrap of grub or water ahead of the operation. I'm a relatively nice person when fed and watered – without either, I transform into a curmudgeonly troll that spits things like 'You wouldn't understand' and 'I don't want to talk about it' when I really do.

Our scheduled section was due at 9 a.m. but a few emergencies had bumped us down the list. It was 7.45 p.m. when I wept to the midwife: 'I either want a sandwich or a baby.'

Having given up on Christmas – *hanger* had replaced any giddy excitement – I made Matt pay for an extortionate TV subscription on the hospital box. A particularly lewd episode of *Family Guy* popped up and we both just stared at the screen, side by side in one of those hospital beds definitely made for one.

I started to turn my focus towards sandwiches. I knew

there was a small supermarket shop in the hospital foyer that closed at 9 p.m., so we'd just about have time to cobble together a cracking ham and cheese double decker with some mustard, perhaps, and a side of salt and vinegar crinkle-cut crisps. The salivation was off the charts and I was about to stampede to the supermarket in a carb-deprived fug when the nurse stopped me in my tracks and said, 'Let's go, they're ready for you.'

This had come just after Peter from *Family Guy* had farted on Greased-up Deaf Guy's head. I didn't know whether my mind was in the right place for bringing life into this world. Matt looked petrified; he'd done a spunk and a baby might happen.

I was the last operation of the day and was swiftly wheeled into theatre with Matt flailing behind, scrambling into white scrubs as he went. He was a far cry from *Grey's Anatomy*'s McDreamy (the surgical beefcake who gave me the right horn in that first trimester). He looked like a confused dinner lady.

The green screens went up and my palms grew intensely sweaty. I don't know at what point I'd lost sight of being cut open and having a baby hauled out of my abdomen. I was vaguely aware of the process but hadn't really connected with the fact this was major abdominal surgery. It's never too late to have a full-on panic attack - complete with all-consuming nausea. It was a case of chunder or cry, which was quite the predicament for Matt, who always tends to need clear instructions. He stood there with a grey cardboard kidney dish, stroking my barnet while simultaneously looking wild-eyed and furrow-browed.

'Can you feel this?' asked the surgeon.

There was some kind of jiggling movement below the screen but I couldn't feel a thing.

After more hoiking and what seemed like an army of heads face down around my nethers, Matt – against my clear instructions 'not to go south' – popped his head over the great divide and tearily mouthed, 'She's here.' He had a gurning smile across his chops that I'd only ever seen at 4 a.m. in a dodgy mosh pit in Camden. He looked like the happiest, most terrified man alive.

He brought this little gunk-encrusted vole to my side and I cried. I cried with relief. I cried with hormones. I cried with nausea. I cried with exhaustion. I cried with hunger. And I cried with pure unadulterated happiness that I'd made a human with another human I loved very much.

I cried because after three very difficult years, I was going to be able to write 'mother' on a form at some point.

No one can tell you what it feels like to bring life into this world. Despite being one of earth's most popular activities, that journey to splashdown will come with so many personal meandering twists and turns that no births can ever be the same.

All I do know is that it's the beginning of something that has you thinking of someone else instead of yourself. Be that a good or bad thing, it's a different thing. Your life of whiling away Sundays on the sofa wondering if you have the energy to pop to the corner shop for some Ben & Jerry's is gone. In its place is a world of wonder and worry as you find yourself asleep, dribbling on the carpet with the Sleep Sheep hissing its 'soothing' white noise in the distance. It's a world where you feel woefully unprepared at every turn – because despite all the weighty tomes dotted about the bookshelves, there's no one who can tell you exactly how your one will work.

As you sit there riddled with hormonal happiness, there's no consideration for the time ahead. Unlike A-levels, where you go through months of preparation on micro- and macro-economic factors, over in Procreation Studies you're handed a pink wailing mass with the instruction: 'Keep it alive'. It's the single most exhilarating and terrifying moment of your life.

Once I'd been stitched up and Matt had transformed from confused dinner lady to the man I know and love, we were wheeled back onto the maternity ward. *Family Guy* was paused on the bit where Greased-up Deaf Guy is running about post-head-fart. It seemed like a lifetime ago. In many ways the previous thirty-nine minutes had been on standstill as we brought Mae into this world with the help of a tray of surgical sharp goods.

I don't know whether I expected an instant bond or not. I was definitely relieved we'd got this one to home base, but I could also see that she resembled a miniature Matt. She looked like a grumpy old Scottish man who had just been denied a packet of pork scratchings in his local. My maternal joy did not blind me. It's certainly not something to worry about – a friend of mine said her daughter looked like the actor Simon

Pegg for the first three months. Another felt her son had a hint of Barbra Streisand to him. They all even out eventually – it's possibly why Pampers tends to only cast four-month-olds and up.

Also, if your baby has a shock of gorilla-like hair coursing down his or her back, fear not, it's normal.

When my sister arrived on the ward the next morning, the physical pain of that C-section instantly made itself known. The one thing that causes a whole world of issues post-partum is laughter. However the baby exited the maternal hutch, laughter will be the biggest test for your urinary tract/stitches/ pain threshold.

It started when the nurse asked if I wanted to try breast pumping. My sister, Karen, arrived just after I'd had those little yellow funnels strapped to each boob. Looking back, there was a hint of Madonna's *Vogue* video – complete with gold conical bra – to the whole scene. Except I had a catheter and sported the pasty pallor and sunken eyes of a recovering heroin addict.

My sister could not stop laughing. The laughter was infectious and the pain was intense. Karen was asked to leave the room while I 'recovered'. She tried entering the room a further two times to catastrophic effect. It was like being told off in school assembly for laughing when Mrs Jones at the piano let out a trump. It was absolute torture but all worth it because it had been an intense twenty-four hours and a bit of perspective was needed. We would be okay; the baby would be okay. Laughter continues to be my preferred tonic in times of maternal strife.

Karen changed her first nappy and there was a lot of heavy breathing and wide-eyed questions about why the poo was mustard-hued. I think the nurse was keen to give her a job to save having to re-stitch my abdomen. After freaking out a little when clapping eyes on the 'peg' that holds the remnants of the umbilical cord, Karen took to aunty-ing like a flapping duck to water.

That was the moment my sister and Mae would become the Ren and Stimpy of our family. To this day it's the single most eye-moistening union I've stumbled across as a mother. Parents and grandparents get a lot of the day-to-day glory but seeing 'Aunty Daz' (Mae could never pronounce 'Kaz') galloping through a packed high street as 'orsey' with Mae laughing like a loon is a joyous thing indeed.

Perhaps the most useful thing post-splashdown was my inability to do anything. It forced me to hand over to my folks, sister and Matt as I recovered from being manhandled down below. As someone who likes an element of control and definitely has a 'way' of doing things – cushion arrangement; supermarket orders; TV remote control positioning – it was healthy that I was the last one to the newborn party. By that point Matt was a dab hand and I couldn't edge in with barbed comments such as, 'Did you even *use* Sudocrem?'

Then came the actual start of it all. Parenting. 'So you're being signed out, you are free to go.' Those were the simple words on day three that meant we were being released into the wilds. It was time to take to the task at hand: keeping the small human alive.

Those 'magical' moments

These are quotes from friends of mine about their first moments as a mum. Some names have been changed . . .

'When I had my daughter, my husband didn't know that babies are usually born face down, and as Edie was born he screamed: "OH MY GOD, SHE DOESN'T HAVE A FACE."'

Jane, thirty-five, mother of Edie and Margot.

'I remember being asked a lot about the mucus plug. "Have you seen the mucus plug yet?" I just needed the nurse to stop saying those two words, really.'

Danielle, thirty-two, mother of Dan.

'I read somewhere that ages ago they used to knock mothers out completely during childbirth with methadone. As I was straining my son out through a small vaginal hole, I am sure I wondered how we had regressed so much.'

Claire, thirty, mother of Wrenn.

'I just remember being consumed by the feeling that I needed to leave the hospital. I was 9 cm and the baby was crowning and I just had to get out of there.'

Steph, thirty-four, mother of David.

'I made it clear my husband wasn't going "down there". He listened but the midwife found our camera and started snapping away without us realising. About three weeks later we downloaded all the photos and it was like seeing a car crash. Make. It. Stop.'

Mary, thirty-five, mother of Bella and Joe.

'There was a photo of me holding gas and air in one hand and a roast dinner in the other. The midwife had said I wasn't allowed any food and I disagreed.'

Kat, twenty-nine, mother of Marnie.

'I hated one midwife and loved the other one. It was based on absolutely nothing other than lack of sleep and a slight loss of mind. I also hated my husband and the cheese strings he bought me as a snack.'

Jas, thirty-eight, mother of Magda.

'My midwife was called Janet Jackson. I couldn't get over it. I laughed so much it was awkward. She just said, "Yes, it is."'

Jules, thirty-seven, mother of Mandy.

'I had my legs in stirrups (which I found pretty comfy) after having given birth to our daughter. There was an unfortunate reflection behind the nurse. I watched my engorged vagina being injected and sewn together.'

Allison, thirty-one, mother of Leila.

Papa Pukka.

When the call came, we were watching *Family Guy*. I'd spent €5 on four hours of hospital pay TV, and baby Stewie had developed a tan that he thought might be leading to terminal cancer. The casual mockery of life and death seemed oddly appropriate and slightly surreal.

I was squeezed into the high-sided hospital bed with Anna, feeling like a yeti forced into an occupied one-person canoe.

We'd been mentally prepared since waking at 7 a.m. that morning.

Halfway through our pregnancy our Dutch doctors had advised us that a Caesarean would be safest and we'd booked our slot as casually as a trip to the chiropodist. Anna had called me one afternoon at work to say, 'They can do Thursday 20th or Friday 21st, which is actually the difference between Gemini and Cancer.'

Her sudden belief in Zodiac signs was a worrying revelation, but I put it down to excess oestrogen.

'Friday means I'll use less holiday,' I said, and we were set.

But our 9 a.m. slot was pushed to 10 a.m. then 12, then 'later' as emergencies came in to the operating theatre. I'd felt focused for most of the day, trying to keep calm but muscles a little tense. It felt like the moments before a big presentation or a wedding speech. One where you're pretty confident in what you're going to say, but have lingering doubts about how the audience will react to that joke about the groom's tendency to wet the bed when drunk.

Except of course this didn't last a few moments, it lasted eleven hours. And those lingering doubts are a little more significant, because this is an operation and there will be blood and a surgeon and risks to two lives.

My usual role on our hospital trips was to fetch snacks, but given that Anna couldn't eat, I was mostly there to provide light entertainment and a partner for games of Top Trumps. They told us the theatre closed at 8 p.m., after which we would be bumped to the next day and Anna could have dinner. As the clock crept up to 7.50 p.m. there was a pale amber glow coming through the windows as the sun edged down. The tension was easing away at the prospect of a hot meal and one more night's sleep.

I was saying something inane about Saturday's child working hard for a living as a nurse strode in and, with the matter-of-factness of a railway station Tannoy announcement said, 'So, we have a space and in thirty minutes you'll have a baby.' And then we were very much awake again.

I partly wanted to say, 'Nah, you're all right, tomorrow's fine', but did not articulate this sentiment. Instead Anna and I smiled. We looked at each other and laughed and said, 'Okay', because we didn't know what else to do.

I think that life's most significant moments stay in your memory because you don't quite believe them and want them to stop.

On the day we got married, at the moment I looked back at Anna as she appeared at the head of the aisle, I wanted the world to pause. I wanted the planet to take a breath so I could burn a picture onto my retina to re-view in those flashing scenes before the end. I wanted someone to tell me that it was real.

And in the same way, the sadder moments are fixed there because I wanted someone to tell me they were a lie. Like the moment I looked up at a row of mourners waiting to shake my hand at my dad's cremation and wondered why I'd only seen him twice in the past ten years. Or aged fifteen in a dark hospital room, holding the hand of my maternal granddad just a couple of weeks after he'd taught me to shave and a few days before he'd die, when he couldn't speak or move but was pleading with his eyes, trying to tell me something that he never managed to say.

And so as the orderly pushed Anna's bed through a corridor and I trotted alongside, I wanted them to slow down. I wanted to get a better grip on her hand as we navigated doorways and other beds. I wanted someone to tell me that this was happening. I would look down at Anna and then up at the path ahead and tell myself, 'This wall is yellow' or, 'We're on the fifth floor' or, 'The orderly looks tired' – anything to etch it into my mind. And then we were in a side room next to the theatre and I was getting into scrubs.

I had been excited about this moment as I thought it'd be a bit like being a doctor. Who needs seven years of medical school when you can just wear green scrubs and hold your hands in the air like you're about to patch up some internal organs? I secretly expected Anna to swoon on seeing me in a surgeon's garb. And then I saw what I'd be wearing: not green surgical gear but a papery white bodysuit complete with hood. Seems only the pros get the good kit and I was resigned to a substitute's bib. It was like the Borehamwood and Herts Under-13 Cup Final all over again.

I like to think that in spite of this I looked like the dad

from *Breaking Bad* at the peak of his badassery. But with hindsight, the pictures suggest I looked more like a permanent in-patient at a facility that serves dinner with rubber cutlery.

The obstacle in scrubs

During the business end of the birthing process, the partner is both important and inconvenient. You are there as a friendly face and encouraging soulmate, but you are also a colossal obstacle in scrubs. A 'scrubstacle', if you will.

Everyone in the room has a very important and specific task to perform. In a C-section there will be up to half a dozen highly trained medical professionals, from the knife-wielding obstetrician to the surgical tech. In a vaginal birth, the room is slightly less crowded but still likely to carry at least a decade of medical training and many more years of practical experience.

The partner's job is to breathe properly, hold hands and make caring noises. If it wasn't a massive hygiene breach, a well-trained Labrador could do it.

But the importance of this role is more spiritual than practical. You are there to provide the sensation of control, like a toy steering wheel strapped to the back of the driver's seat in a car. In this analogy, you are the eager toddler in the back seat, convinced that every twist of the wheel is vitally important. The grown-ups (the medical team) just want you to make happy noises and not cry too much.

Depending on whether you are having a C-section or a vaginal birth, these are the setups you will probably encounter:

C Team

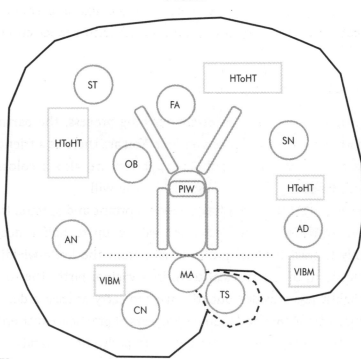

KEY

···· Screen

– – Pocket of emotional enrichment

— **NO-FLY ZONE**

EQUIPMENT

HToHT – Hostess trolley of hospital things (like off of *ER/Casualty*)

VIBM – Very important bleepy machine (monitors life signs)

PEOPLE

OB – Obstetrician (big chief)

FA – First assistant nurse (2-IC)

AD – Anaesthetic doctor (gas piper)

AN – Anaesthetic nurse (gas checker)

SN – Scrub nurse (washer up)

ST – Surgical tech (stuff fetcher)

CN – Circulator nurse (internal comms)

MA – Main attraction (star of the show)

PIW – Person-in-waiting (baby)

TS – The scrubstacle (partner)

V Team (hospital)

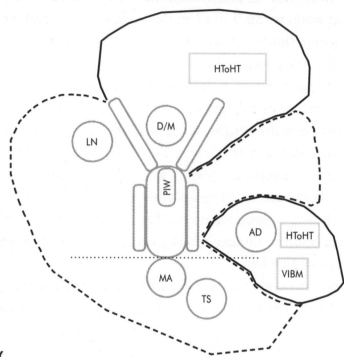

KEY
···· Screen
-- Pocket of emotional enrichment
— **NO-FLY ZONE**

EQUIPMENT
HToHT – Hostess trolley of hospital things (like off of *ER/Casualty*)
VIBM – Very important bleepy machine (monitors life signs)

PEOPLE
D/M – Doctor or midwife (catcher)
LN – Labour nurse (2-IC)
AD – Anaesthesiologist (drug dealer optional)
MA – Main attraction (star of the show)
PIW – Person-in-waiting (baby)
TS – The scrubstacle (partner)

In the first plan, you will notice there is a significant no-fly zone where medical professionals do their bit. Meanwhile, the partner works within a small 'pocket of emotional enrichment', saying nice things, holding the pregnant person's hand and generally being awed by the imminent arrival of a new life. You also get to sit on a bar stool on wheels.

Your oracle in this process is the circulator nurse. He or she will be monitoring signs, keeping the surgeon informed and answering any of your questions. In that time you may start to look upon them like a beloved aunt or uncle, but it's best to hold back on the hugs until afterwards.

The hospital set-up for a vaginal birth (facing page) is much simpler, and the thinner crowd gives the partner much more scope to be involved.

Births at home can be even more sparsely attended: just mum-to-be, partner and a midwife (plus pool and fishing net).

●

There was a thin arc of blood as they made the first incision, and Anna asked me not to look. For all that we knew of each other after six years together, peeking inside her womb seemed an intimacy too far.

The screen was raised above her neck and we stared dumbly at each other as the medical team buzzed around like a well-practised pit crew, wheeling monitors on trolleys and chatting in calm but focused Dutch. I felt a little like I do whenever I travel on a small plane: rigid with fear but trying to enjoy the ride, convinced that leaning one way or the other will cause a crash, but trying to appear worldly and at ease.

She had been anaesthetised and was relaxed but a little uncomfortable. I asked if she could feel anything and she gave a grimace. We stared at each other and smiled and I occasionally kissed her hand, and again I felt disbelief. I wanted it to be over, to know that all was well and Anna was out of danger, but I also wanted it to stop – I wanted the world to freeze so I could look around and have someone tell me it was real.

Every couple of minutes the circulator nurse would speak in English to tell us that everything was fine. Steadily the Dutch medical chatter increased: the pace picked up, the tone grew sterner and the surgeon switched to English.

'Hey, your baby's coming; don't you want to look?'

I stood up and there she was: blue and slimy, skin all bunched up like an old sock. Grizzly and perfect.

I laughed and wept as she gave her first cries and gasps for air. They held her high as she squirmed, and then presented her to Anna like 2 kg of topside won in a pub meat raffle. I glanced at the nurses and the doctor for any worried expressions, but there were just professional smiles.

She was placed precariously on Anna's shoulder and we held her there and cried and laughed some more. Then they took her away and asked me to follow. She was weighed and checked beneath a little heater and they handed me the surgical scissors. The sub's moment had come to step off the bench.

From an early age we are taught to take care with sharp

implements and told that playing with knives might cost a digit.

So slicing through a body part – however temporary a body part it's meant to be – went against my natural instincts. The umbilical cord is blue and rubbery and in those first few moments much of the baby is blue too. Even once the nurse had placed the cord between the blades I stood there dumbly and said, 'This bit, yeah? Definitely this bit?'

It had the consistency of overcooked calamari but I made the slice. Technically I had just performed surgery, and I stepped back like a puffed-up city councillor after a ribbon cutting for a library that he had no part in building.

They put a bonnet on Mae, wrapped her up like a spring roll and we returned to Anna.

The rest fits in flashes of memory. This would be the moment in a 1980s film where they'd show a montage of Polaroids. Here's us in a recovery room with Mae taking her first feed as we gawp in love-struck wonder. Here's us back on the ward, Anna laid low by her surgery and Mae beneath my hoody, her head on my naked chest for the bonding of skin-on-skin contact. Here's Matt giving the first bath in a metal sink while Mae's unadjusted eyes peer up at blobs of light.

And then I cycled home. Visitors couldn't stay overnight, Anna needed rest and Mae was in the crib by her bedside, so I was packed off, stone-cold sober but emotionally tripping my tits off. It was about 1 a.m. and my rickety Dutch 'granddad bike' clanked along the quiet streets, over the river Amstel and home to our flat.

I sat in the room that was waiting for Mae and wondered how the next bit might be. I wondered if I should drink less and get life insurance (or any insurance, come to that). I wondered if we'd do swimming lessons every Saturday and how you brush a baby's teeth. I wondered how bad the teenage years would be and what sort of relationship might remain afterwards. I wondered if she'd be bookish or brazen, creative or clinical, who she'd meet and what she'd do. And I wondered whether I'd be able to keep her safe.

I sat on the daybed that we'd squeezed in to take up about a quarter of Mae's room, and felt the odd sensation of knowing that our world had changed for ever but that it all looked just the same.

Two ways out

So: *au naturel* or through the sunroof? Hard drugs or wild-eyed determination? There's more than one way to let your tiny life into the world, and each has pros and cons.

NATURAL BIRTH

Vaginal births remain the most common way to release your offspring into the wild. This is how it's been done for a millennium or several, and medical science tends to point mums this way where possible. For the mother, while there may be tearing – yikes – the recovery time is much shorter than with a Caesarean, and you will usually only need to stay for one night. In some countries, the mother is sent home the same day.

It generally means the child is born when it's ready and with lungs fully developed, rather than a week or two before the due date if it's a planned C-section. Some studies have suggested this can mean a slightly lower chance of respiratory problems.

The trip through the birth canal also stimulates the baby's cardiovascular system, provides protective bacteria that help the immune system as they grow and provides a surge of feel-good hormones that can make them more likely to breastfeed and to feel connected to their mother.

On the downside are the tearing, stitches and potential injury to pelvic muscles that control the bowels.
Yikes again. Labour takes on average about eight hours
but can last much longer, and ends with a euphoric
hormone surge that is thought to help with bonding in
the immediate aftermath.

CAESAREAN
About one in four births in the UK are a C-section,
where a cut of about 10–20 cm will be made across the
lower tummy and womb so the baby can be delivered.
Typically these are emergency C-sections to conclude a
difficult natural birth, or a planned C-section because
of a high risk from natural birth, and following
medical advice.

A Caesarean tends to mean less damage on the way
out, but remains a serious operation. Despite the
epidural, mothers often feel some tugging during the
procedure. The first few days afterwards can be very
painful as the wound heals and they normally require
a hospital stay of three or four days. You are also
advised against strenuous activity and heavy lifting for
about six weeks afterwards. The operation takes about
forty-five minutes.

Home or hospital

This largely comes down to you. There are ardent advocates of both, but with a low-risk birth, it's about your own preference – do you want to get dressed up and eat out, or have a takeaway at home with the lighting and mood exactly as you want them, but the significant downside that you'll also have to do the washing-up (and there is a lot of washing-up)?

In 2011, *The British Medical Journal* released the biggest study into home versus hospital births in the UK, looking at 64,538 cases where women gave birth at full term. The good news was that, generally, births at home, in hospital and in midwife units all carried a low level of risk.

For first-time mums the chances of complications during a home birth were three times higher than in a hospital birth. 'Complications' in this case means mortality, broken bones, nerve injury, brain injury and respiratory infection.

While this sounds like a dramatic increase, the chances of complications remain low.

For first-time mums who had their child at home, there were complications in 75 births out of 8,551 – that's 11.4 per 1,000.

Across all pregnancies, there were complications in 4.3 births in every 1,000.

In second or subsequent births, there was no significant difference in the risks.

One thing to note, in the swirling and contradictory turd-vortex of misinformation thrown at parents, is how different newspapers covered the same report, with stories that ranged from sober to scaremongering. These headlines are from 25 November 2011:

'First-time mothers warned over home birth risks'

Daily Telegraph

'Women with low-risk pregnancies "should have birth choices"'   *Guardian*

'First-time mothers who opt for home birth face triple the risk of death or brain damage in child'

Daily Mail

'Home as safe as hospital for second births'

Independent

'Home births three times more risky than hospital, says study'   *Metro*

'Home birth risks up for new mums'   *Sun*

So speak to your doctor and then decide what feels right for you. You can find the full report by searching BMJ.com for 'Perinatal and maternal outcomes by planned place of birth'.

6

The instructions don't work

Mother Pukka.

I've had five hamsters and, despite all my best efforts, none of them lasted long, so I had a legitimate fear of being a mother. While wildly different in aesthetic, hamsters have the same ability as a newborn to keep you up into the dead of night with relentless whirring and clattering that is hard to decode.

My dad said you can't win in those first few months: if they're crying blue murder, you're willing them to stop. Once they are quiet, you're wide-eyed and worried that they're not breathing or that Sophie La Girafe has become a choking hazard.

I think the moment I first became a parent was three weeks after Mae was born – when all the initial excitement had died down. The time before that was wonderfully hazy, oxytocin-fuelled and full of flowers and other lovely frippery that made everything okay. It's when The Stuff stops coming, the homemade frozen dinners run out, the elephant-sized fanny pads stop being needed and you realise you have to keep this small mite alive for ever – without clear instructions – that parenting starts.

It was 32 degrees and I was trapped in a stifling Amsterdam apartment. I was crying, a newborn Mae was hollering – the sort of squawking that has social services perking up – and our beagle Douglas was whimpering about his life choices. He did not seem as keen to see our DNA in small human form as we were – there was definitely a growling hint of sibling rivalry lurking.

I had lost all sense of day or night and a lurking resentment was building about Matt's ability to 'sleep through the night' when everyone else was a gibbering wreck. That included Douglas, who seemed aghast about the whole situation and looked at Mae like a Friday-night drunk might look at a kebab.

Looking back, Matt was just as frazzled as I was but did what he's always done in times of emotional imbalance – got on with things with a British resilience I've always admired. For every gripe I'd offer up about him not understanding my unravelling mind, he'd respond with, 'It will be okay; we will be okay.'

I didn't feel okay. I felt lost in a sea of misinformation and started wildly panic-buying things with the word 'miracle' in them from eBay. Anything to stop the relentless crying that seemed impossible to sate with boob, dummy, teddy, shushing or wobbly lullaby.

I looked at photos of fresh-faced mothers on the internet cuddling their newborns and it seemed like my one was broken.

I called my mate down the road who was bed-bound after a tricky birth herself and she simply said: 'Grab something booze-based and get your pillowy ass over here.'

I did as I was told and we sipped warm wine from a plastic IKEA child's beaker. I pumped my boobs to within an inch of their sorry lives to ensure Mae wasn't getting drunk at three weeks old with my sullied breastmilk. I cried a bit about being a horrible mother and I cried about the plastic green beaker – it was a sorry scene. Then I remember thinking: it's not going to be easy, this parenting thing, but there will always be a way forward.

And that was it. As Mae hit three weeks, I stopped trying to be a yummy mummy, a mombie, a mum even. It didn't matter how much I pinned to my Pinterest board; I put the books down and eased myself off the forums, reasoning in that snot-embellished moment that I wasn't going to be one of those lucky ones breezily wafting about in a white kaftan, her baby in one arm, her Kegel exercise app open in the other.

I'd find myself ricocheting from Gina Ford-championing capable mother to irrational banshee. Every day was a hormonal rollercoaster with my wobbly lower lip always ready to go full codfish. But that was okay.

Whether you're an eco-mum, strapping that life burden to you as you downward-dog the madness away, or a manic cupcake-baker, hoping that each pastel-hued confection will piece together a little of your mind, the only thing I (and Frank Sinatra) know is, there is only one way: yours.

There are those who slap Lady Danger lipstick on to detract

from the blood-shot eyes of those first few months. There are others who pretend their lives haven't changed a jot, but are a veritable weeping mess behind the scenes (complete with spiky fanny hair regrowth). Then there's the turbo maternal ones who try and help everyone else before helping themselves. There's also those who sip lukewarm wine in children's receptacles.

But once the post-splashdown gifts and flowers ease off and the attention disappears, you really are just a girl standing in front of a mewling infant wanting it to love her – or in darker moments, wanting to love it.

How you go forward at that moment is up to you. My route was a WhatsApp group of NCT-esque mates I'd picked up along the way – from park benches, one pregnancy yoga class and that rogue antenatal class we went to – that covered everything from removal of fanny stitches to an analysis of the latest *Kardashians* episode. (My mate Dita rebranded it National Cunt Therapy, NCT Dutch-style.)

Oh, and then there was the Sleep Sheep.

One night (or possibly day), I drifted off to the tropical setting that this slumber-inducing device offers. I was delirious, Matt continued to sleep steadily through the night – despite Mae's hollering – and I was dreaming of another world that didn't include massive flesh-coloured knickers and a droopy eyelid. But it was in that moment, when those exotic sounds made me think I was dozing after a Full Moon Party in Thailand, that I realised a little bit of papering over the cracks could go a long way.

Sure I might not be able to jet off to Club Tropicana, clutching a Mills & Boon novel. But the next day, I booked in for a Vitamin C facial, pumped my boobs until they resembled empty Capri-Sun pouches and handed Mae over to Matt for all of sixty-four minutes. I then went and bought myself a necklace with 'Mama' on it (because even though I wasn't feeling like a very good one, branding is everything).

It was enough. Shallow? Indulgent? Who cares, I went home that day a much nicer person – which was as good for me as it was for my poor family. I decided there was more fun to be had with parenthood. Whether you're boob or bottle, Ella's Kitchen or Annabel Karmel, mum-boss or mum-don't-give-a-toss, it was my mama mates and their perilous tales of parenting that made everything okay. It was stories of 'I found a teaspoon in my kid's nappy' or 'Does anyone else's nipple look like a Jaffa Cake?' that made me see the lighter side and start to realise I wasn't the only one bungling along.

My parental method isn't textbook, it's more 'have a go'. Like my style isn't thought-out, it's more 'stuff that's not in the wash'. But I realised that it's not about what everyone else is doing, it's about what we, as parents, can do together. For me that has always been laughing through the madness. Oh, and remembering a previous life being hungover on a beach in Koh Pha Ngan – and realising that motherhood is, in fact, a much happier place.

Then came the juggernaut of a question from my sister, Karen, which no one had asked yet: 'All okay with you?'

Well, yeah it was until you asked that question and made

me think about it and unleashed an Alton Towers log flume of tears. She asked the question and I cried, simply because I wasn't sure of the answer. I remember I was in some achingly hipster brunch gaff and there was a general sense of worry in the air from all the moustachioed patrons: 'Why are there parent-people here? This is not a parent-people place.'

Doubt is a cruel mistress. She's a wily sort who edges into your thoughts at 3.14 a.m. when there's nothing but Instagram posts from lithe Californian girls on skateboards for company. It sidles up to you in the dairy aisle of Asda and queries (oh so quietly but ever so clearly) if it's lactose that's causing those piercing newborn screams.

It makes you question boobs, bottle and everything in between. Are my norks limp duds or is she getting enough food? How can I be solely responsible for food supply for something so important? I think, however you choose to feed that kid, the old mantra 'fed is best' rings true. Put the internet down and allow your maternal antenna to perk up on matters of getting food in the kid and don't get sucked into any group discussing the merits of 'boob vs bottle' – if in doubt, call the midwife.

I remember finding myself so exhausted in those first few weeks that I stood in the fruit and veg aisle with Mae strapped to me, unable to move, clutching a pineapple. I clutched that spiky exotic fruit for dear life for a concerning eleven minutes and all I remember is that I was unsure how to proceed.

Doubt is part of being a parent. Despite knowing you can climb that hulking great parental mountain, something edges over and whispers: 'But did you see how calm Jodi's baby was? Why is yours crying like an angry vole? What are YOU doing wrong? Is my rendition of "Wind the Bobbin Up" on point? Can she even hear me? Why don't I know if she can hear me at four weeks old? Is anyone listening? Am I alone? What *is* a bobbin?'

And then all the whispers amass in one snotty bubble and push you over the raggedy edge. It's only when that snot bubble has burst that you can see doubt for what it really is: a flea on a fly on a rat on a cat on a rare Siberian snow leopard. You are the snow leopard. Never doubt that in those first few days. But also don't feel ashamed of breaking a bit when the flower deliveries come to a halt and you hear a bunch of youths coming back at 3 a.m. in a chemical haze as you massage your mastitis-addled knockers. It will get easier – that is one thing I do know.

My first public transport outing was with Mae at four weeks old. I'd wandered about a bit as my C-section scars healed, but had steered clear of buses and trains because of potential buggy lifting. But at twenty-eight days, I felt the mind and abdominal wounds had healed and I was ready to edge back into society. It wasn't a huge success.

I found myself holding Mae like a rugby ball at a packed tram stop as my over-burdened buggy hurtled towards traffic and dozens of my fellow passangers quietly judged on the sidelines. I had forgotten the brakes and I had packed everything but the kitchen sink in the underbelly of that buggy. The steriliser was there, snugly packed between seventeen nappies for Mae and a book for me. (A book? Ah yes. The true stamp of a first-time parent.)

I had a sweat on and grapes falling from my bag. But somehow I steered that buggy back on track and even deposited the rogue vine fruit into a bin so as not to have any litter-bug guilt hanging over me.

And in that bungling moment I realised we're stronger than we could ever imagine. Navigating public transport with a newborn on one-hour-thirteen-minutes' sleep with a relentlessly leaky boob made me feel like I was made of nails.

That was until I was hit by an overwhelming surge one morning of 'Oh my God, what have I done?' It wasn't in relation to the huge life project that was snuffling at my boob (that bit was a massive privilege despite the knackeredness); it was the realisation that I'd been a goon towards my mother, for more than thirty-two years.

I'm sure I had been nice at points over those three decades but the overriding feeling that dawned on me then was that she'd done all this – kept me alive, nurtured me, guided me, loved me, wiped my bum and sourced blackout curtains when I failed – and I'd basically repaid her by stropping about.

I unburdened my heavy maternal heart on the phone the next day. There were tears. I was sorry, but she once again made everything okay, saying, 'Your dad and I wouldn't have wanted one that did everything by the book – that would have worried us more.'

My mum is the first to push the sentiment, 'Do it, go your own way; it's not selfish, it's honest.' And she'd always wrap my sandwiches up in a way that stood out (think a foil swan extravagance) from the packed-lunch crowd.

In those early days with Mae, she'd given me the advice that kept my mind strung together: 'Sometimes it is okay to shut the door on the screaming child and have a cup of tea. Sometime you must put the kettle on and give yourself a break – before you actually break.'

And that's actually the advice I'd give to mothers in their first month: give yourself a break, before you actually break, and ask for help if things feel too hard. That, and don't under-estimate the power of TENA Lady Pants.

More stuff they don't tell you

HAIRY TIMES
Mae's hair fell out after three weeks. She had sideburns and looked a bit like Mr Burns off *The Simpsons*. This can happen and it will grow back, but a bold hat always balances out that old-man aesthetic.

BROWN-EYED GIRL
Babies are born with blue eyes. I congratulated myself that Mae had my eyes until they changed to brown. I thought I'd lost my mind somewhere in the tinned goods aisle when I first noticed.

UP CLOSE AND PERSONAL
You need to be 20 to 38 cm from the nipper's nose to get any sense of recognition. That expensive baby jungle you bought isn't going to get a look-in for a few months.

JITTER BUG
That weird shuddering – arms flailing, fists wide, knees up – that babies sometimes do is called a Moro reflex. When Mae first did it I thought she was having a 'turn' and wanted to call an ambulance.

DON'T CRY ME A RIVER
Despite the wailing, Mae didn't actually produce any tears and I thought she had severe dehydration. I called my doctor and apparently the tear ducts aren't fully developed that early, so proper tears won't roll for a few weeks.

THE SOUND OF MUSIC
Babies recognise songs they hear in the womb for up to four months after birth, according to University of Helsinki research. There's a dad who practised Buddhist *omming* while his kid was in the womb. Once born, it always sent her to sleep. That has to be worth a go.

SPOT OF BOTHER

Mae had loads of whiteheads on her face and I was tempted to pick one. It feels tempting to sort them out, but hold back. It can cause scarring and you don't need to feel more guilt every time you look at your kid's face.

ZONE OUT

In fact, at first he/she will only really be alert for around three minutes in every hour during the day, and even less at night. It's not you; it's him/her.

HAVE A WHIFF

For you, anyway. A University of Montreal study looked at the brains of fifteen new mums and found the smell of a newborn brought out the same pleasure and sense of craving that food does when we're hungry. If you find yourself falling apart, have a cuppa and a whiff of that bonce.

The stuff to do: from random parents we stopped on the internet

Ignore unwanted or confusing advice. 'In the end, you're the parents, so you decide what's best,' says Julie of Wandsworth.

'Forget about housework for the first couple of months,' says Jane of Wigan. 'Concentrate on getting to know your baby. If anyone has anything to say about the dust piling up or the unwashed dishes, smile and hand them a duster or the washing-up liquid.'

Accept help from anyone who is nice – or naive – enough to offer. 'If a neighbour wants to hold the baby while you shower, say yes,' says Jeanne of Stratford.

Got lots of people who want to help but don't know how? 'Don't be afraid to tell people exactly what you need,' says Abby of Liverpool. 'It's one of the few times in your life when you'll be able to order everyone around.'

But don't give other people the small jobs. 'Changing a nappy takes two minutes. You'll need others to do time-consuming work like cooking, sweeping floors and buying nappies,' says Catherine of Aberystwyth.

Reconnect. To keep yourself from feeling detached from the world, Louise from Manchester, suggests: 'Get outside on your own, even for five minutes.'

Papa Pukka.

My first moments alone with Mae felt like a terrible mistake. I was someone who couldn't drive, was intimidated by changing light bulbs, and who *always* forgot to buy toilet paper. Anna had a history of accidentally burning things with hair tongs and had been overdrawn for most of her adult life. It seemed deeply irresponsible that we would be left in sole charge of this tiny creature, and I hoped the authorities would send more help. Having a state-provided Dutch maternity nurse with us for the first week at home didn't seem enough. Each time I woke and Mae was silent I would creep up to her crib to check that she was still breathing. Those tiny breaths were so fragile it seemed impossible that her chest could rise after it fell.

But slowly, a basic level of understanding crept in. Much like an iPad, a baby appears miraculous and mysterious at first, but operating them is actually quite intuitive. If in doubt, just swipe about until something works (by which I mean feed, burp, change or cuddle – actual swiping is not encouraged). As with full-sized humans, the quickest steps to contentment are usually sleep or food.

The first three months are sometimes referred to as the 'fourth trimester', despite the fact that the bambino has escaped the womb. This is because after nine months in the warm, cocoon-like haze, the fresh air and open spaces come as a bit of a shock, much like when they turn on the lights in a club and boot you out into the cold.

Cannier mammals than humans can walk, see and hear from the moment they are born, but we go through a period of adjustment. One theory – the 'obstetrical dilemma' – suggests that this is an evolutionary flaw and gestation should be longer. As we edged from scrabbling around on all fours to walking upright, our pelvises became narrower. But we also had to become clever enough to invent things like the wheel and pine-scented cardboard trees, so our brains (and skulls) were growing bigger at the same time. This created a bit of a sizing issue, one having to pass through the other, so we started popping out a little sooner. Non-human primates arrive with about 45 to 50 per cent brain development, while we manage just 25 per cent, the bunch of divs that we are. Essentially, evolution is a work in progress and a compromise has been made on gestation periods, which is why newborns all look like unripe raisins.

So new babies see the world in blurred patches and can't yet distinguish individual sounds and voices.

For those first few weeks there's no hope of any routine; just provide a steady flow of nappies, milk and cuddles. And there's not much else to do, other than sleep when you can and get outside where possible, though that was easier for me than for Anna.

C-sections involve pulling apart the abdominal muscles. It was forty-eight hours before Anna could sit herself up, and even then there was significant pain. She spent the first four nights in hospital, which meant I could spend the day with her and Mae and then go home to sleep. It was a warm summer of late sunsets in Amsterdam, and on the way home I would sit alone on the terrace of a little bar and drink a small beer, wide-eyed with wonder about the following weeks and generally getting my head in order – something I usually find simpler to do alone than, you know, by talking to other humans.

Once Anna was home, we had her recovery to take care of along with our new addition. Women are advised not to do any heaving lifting for the first six weeks after a Caesarean, which is a difficult feat with a newborn in need of constant attention.

So a new chain of command quickly developed, and I found myself in the role of lowly quartermaster NCO. Anna was the general and directed operations from her feeding throne, while Mae was like a crackpot field marshal from the First World War, alternating between quiet contemplation and send-'em-over-the-top rages. Doug the beagle found himself demoted and wasn't happy about it at all.

Along with fetching supplies I did most of the changing in those early days, while Anna rested as much as possible and handled the feeds. When Mae mewled at feeding time, I'd bring her over to Anna, either propped up on the sofa or in our bed, and lay Mae in her arms. Then I'd go and do some work, intermittently being sent to fetch items just out of Anna's reach. My name became, 'Matt could-you-just . . .'

And then the time came to take our little cub out into the wild. After spending her first few days indoors, we decided to give Mae some fresh air. It was a warm summer and our apartment grew stifling by the afternoon. Anna still had some difficulty moving and we were up two flights of stairs, so I scooped up our little parcel and carried her down to the buggy we kept in the communal hallway.

These devices, with their mysterious swivels and clicks, have reduced many a grown man to tears of impotent rage. I'd wheeled ours back from the shop a few weeks before to some slightly confused looks: there is something about a person wheeling an empty buggy through the streets that screams 'colossal mental breakdown', as though I had an imaginary baby in there and possibly also heard the voice of my dead mother squawking from a loft room.*

But now I had a person to put in it, and did so without shearing any digits off either of us. That first walk felt like something I really should not be allowed to do and I expected disaster to occur at any minute: for a roof slate to come crashing down into the buggy, or a car to mount the kerb. I couldn't believe it was legal for me to be let loose with this tiny, delicate thing and I wondered if anyone might intervene. Whenever a stranger looked my way, I expected them to step forward and tell me that I was doing something terribly wrong and might already have caused lifelong damage to this minuscule person.

I turned out of our side street onto a main road. We were living a few hundred metres from the red-light district by then, on a quiet residential street with leafy canals one way and this main road – Vijzelstraat – the other. It had tramlines running down the middle, a steady flow of cars, and a trickle of tourists bumbling along the pavement. I was convinced every one of them was a kidnapper or about to tumble head first into the buggy.

And then I realised how annoying buggies are. I tend to walk in a mildly irritated stride. The pace of pedestrians on a

---

* This is a reference to Norman Bates in *Psycho*. My own dear mum, Paula, is alive and well and in charge of most of her faculties. (Hello Mum! Love you! Sorry if the book's a bit revealing, but I'm told it's what people expect these days. Sometimes I wish I'd just stayed on the wood section at Do It All on Whetstone High Road.)

typical high street feels a bit dawdly, and so I'm constantly overtaking people in that slightly self-important way of people-who-walk-quickly, even if the end goal of my stroll is nothing more than a nice sit-down and a cup of tea.

This rage increases in crowds and approaches a zenith whenever I step into a Tube station, revving up my stride to find the perfect spot on the platform while an imaginary motorsport commentary plays in my head. This hotstepping zeal has caused issues in previous relationships, with at least one former girlfriend, who was constantly left half a pace behind, deciding that we couldn't possibly be meant for each other. I fully agreed.

But this quickstep is impossible with a buggy, particularly on the narrow pavements of Amsterdam. Overtaking is not an option, and I soon found myself silently seething at those strolling in front of us. It was only when I prodded the buggy into the calves of a slightly stoned Italian man that I realised I may have gone too far in using my five-day-old child as a weapon. So I swerved off onto a side street to better enjoy that first walk. I say enjoy: that is apart from the nagging suspicion that at any moment I would lose control of the buggy and watch it roll down a slope into a canal (bear in mind that in Amsterdam this happens to a car on average once a week, and cars have really strong brakes).

But we made it home alive and the first days drifted by in an oddly peaceful, if sleep-deprived, haze of cuddles and changes and milky turds.

I was freelance and had taken two weeks off, but come the

end of that fortnight I was ready to return. The truth is, as full as you may be with love and wonder, newborns are pretty dull.

Tamagotchi theory

New babies provide limited returns. You are their subservient provider and they are incapable of showing the faintest crumb of affection or gratitude in return. The best you can hope for is that they might blindly nuzzle into your neck as they sleep, but even then you are little more than a bony cushion.

They can't smile for at least six months, so won't laugh at any of your jokes or funny faces. They can't tell when you're down, so won't offer hugs or cheer you up with a spontaneous shin cuddle. Their conversation is rubbish and they can't catch. They are there to be catered for and nothing more.

In effect, you now have your own real-life tamagotchi – a Japanese toy craze that briefly swept the UK in the late 1990s and early 2000s. These little plastic, keyring-sized toys had a screen with a blocky digital character on it that would 'hatch' for you to rear. Perhaps the most disturbing thing about the craze was seeing adults play with them as often as children. At least once while walking through my university canteen I heard a fellow student say, 'Awww, Pianitchi's done a poopy!'

With a baby, as with the pocket-pet phenomenon, your role is to provide support on demand, as demonstrated here:

Tamagotchi Theory

TAMAGOTCHI

Indicator	Action	Frequency
Hunger meter	Feed to earn heart icons	Varies: play may be paused
Happy meter	Play to earn heart icons	Varies: play may be paused
Light meter	Turn off bulb for sleep	Varies: play may be paused
Health meter	Address skull icons with medicine	Varies: play may be paused
Duck meter	Clean poop from floor	Varies: play may be paused

ACTUAL BABY

Indicator	Action	Frequency
Crying	Bottle or breast feed	8–12 times a day
Crying	Make goo-goo-gaa-gaa noises/turn on mobile	Short spells for about half of waking time
Crying	Cocoon in cosy pitch-black space for nap	About 18 hours a day in 30-minute to two-hour spells
Crying	Check temperature/call doctor	Rare, hopefully
Crying	Change nappy	With feeds, more if needed

You will notice a few key differences. Bandai Namco Entertainment Inc. has very considerately included a number of meters on tamagotchis, so it's clear exactly what they may need. Human evolution has failed to match this basic indicator system, so all you've got to go by is indistinct crying.

Another significant difference is that, unlike with tamagotchis, there is no pause button on a baby: you are now trapped in an endless cycle of caring and your only escape is gin.

But this is where the genius of the tiny toys – and the essence of tamagotchi theory – becomes clear: the more sustenance you provide, the more committed you become to your tiny charge. You don't get the slightest thanks or praise, but you continue because it feels right and you genuinely begin to care. It's nature's way (and also the Bandai Namco Entertainment Inc. way) of helping you become less selfish and more patient.

Becoming a right soppy bastard

Fathers play a role in rearing in fewer than 6 per cent of mammal species. From antelopes to aardvarks, the dads typically make a deposit then amble off to a watering hole with a smile on their face. So what is it that makes human men more likely to stick around (beyond social stigma and the far-reaching arms of the Child Support Agency)?

First up, the new arrival looks a bit like you (or at least, the unripe raisin version of you),* which is a little bit of evolutionary encouragement to stick around in a world where sharp-toothed predators have been replaced by traffic fumes, small chokable objects and the internet. One long-running theory has it that newborns look much more like their dads than their mums precisely to encourage fathers to stay. But a series of studies in the journal *Evolution & Human Behavior* have poo-pooed this premise, by showing pictures of babies and adults to independent assessors, who correctly matched mothers with their babies as much as they matched fathers with theirs. Even so, be it the curve of the brow or a kink of the nose, there's likely to be something there that you'll recognise, which does make it seem a little trickier to run away to Acapulco.

And then there's the fact that becoming a dad might structurally change your brain. In a 2014 study from the Universities of Denver and Yale, researchers scanned the brains of sixteen new dads at two to four weeks after their babies had been born, and then again twelve to sixteen weeks later. In the later scans, parts of the brain had grown, including the parts associated with hormonal control and emotional processing. But they also noticed that some parts had shrunk. The bits of brain known as the 'default mode network' are the parts that spark up when you are doing nothing. When you switch off from the outside world, the default mode network starts ticking over. For the new dads, these brain parts had shrunk in the later scan. The

---

* This may also be true of aardvarks, but at the risk of being offensively species-ist, they all look the same to me.

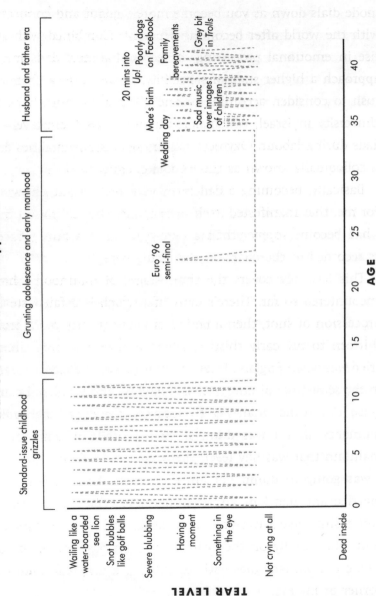

Chart of Post-Parental Ensoppiment

Standard-issue childhood grizzles

Grunting adolescence and early manhood

Husband and father era

TEAR LEVEL

Wailing like a water-boarded sea lion

Snot bubbles like golf balls

Severe blubbing

Having a moment

Something in the eye

Not crying at all

Dead inside

AGE

0 · 5 · 10 · 15 · 20 · 25 · 30 · 35 · 40

Euro '96 semi-final

Wedding day

Mae's birth

20 mins into Up!

Sad music over images of children

Poorly dogs on Facebook

Family bereavements

Grey bit in Trolls

theory, although based on a tiny sample, is that the default mode dials down as you become more vigilant and connected with the world after becoming a parent. Combined with the rise in emotional processing, it seems that new dads might approach a higher state of sensibility. There's also a chemical rush to consider, according to one 2010 study from Bar-Ilan University in Israel, which noted a rise in oxytocin levels in dads during labour. Oxytocin has antidepressant qualities and is colloquially known as the 'cuddle chemical'.

Basically, becoming a dad turns you into a right old wuss. For me, that manifested itself in tears and the realisation that I had become soppier than a four-year-old at a bunny farm, as recorded in the chart on the facing page.

This basically covers the three stages of manhood I have encountered so far. There's early life, which is a fairly steady procession of snot, then a period of about twenty years, from thirteen to my early thirties, where I think the only time I cried was when England lost the penalty shoot-out to Germany in the semi-final of Euro 96. (It might have looked like I came close that time 'Stairway to Heaven' came on the radio, moments after I was dumped by my first girlfriend, but I maintain that was hay fever in my eyes and I didn't care 'cos I was going to dump her anyway, so it's fine.) Then I got married and had kids and the taps have been on ever since. Not gushing like Sylvester Stallone at the end of the first *Rambo* film, but steadily on the cusp. I can't get past the bit in *Up* where the old lady dies without rubbing a tiny tear from the corner of my eye.

I'm a more emotional soul than I've been since childhood, and it feels like most of that can be traced back to the arrival of Mae. When she joined us, I slowly began to think differently. I felt global issues more keenly, aware it was no longer just me they might affect. I am more sensitive to how people treat each other, and in particular how men talk about women. Having a daughter has made me realise how oafishly many men treat women every day (and how I did for most of the middle bit of the chart).

Since the moment Mae arrived, whenever she's out of sight I feel unease and wonder if all is okay. If I'm at work and she's at nursery, I feel sudden peaks of worry and want to see what she's doing at that precise moment. It's like that urge you get to check for your passport when you're in an airport, but without the promise of a Bloody Mary and in-flight film.

There is a steady, low-level worry ticking away at the back of my mind. It could become overwhelming if allowed to, but it's good that it's there because without it I'm not sure any bond would exist. And without that bond of soppiness, that endless well of gormless love, I'm not sure how I'd have got through the months that followed.

7

Work hard, play hard

Mother Pukka.

I was, I think, a bad person in the first year of Mae's life. I would seethe as a mate's kid started sleeping through the night while mine was a foghorn from 2 a.m. to 6 a.m. I was so tired I couldn't see the judgemental wood from the friendly trees.

I remember the moment things got really bad when I started 'tutting'. Like, I'd tut at someone clogging up the pavement so I couldn't wheel Mae past in the manner of a sozzled stag-do attendee on a go-kart track.

Each baby sensory class I attended made the internal 'tuts' louder. I went with mate-whose-child-was-sleeping-through-the-night to this class every Tuesday at 9.15 a.m. Mae was three months at this point and I was still fairly sure she wasn't cognitively all there – some people's babies seemed to be smiling and chirping in response to their doting mums, while Mae just looked angry and quizzical. But I pressed on because everyone else seemed to be doing the right thing, sitting in a community hall that smelt of feet, but probably secretly willing the tambourine to stop.

The day I cracked was when the lady running the class got up in my grill and started singing, 'Say hello to the sun, shining over me, you are the sun and you bring light to me.' She accompanied this ditty with flailing arm movements and a slice-of-watermelon smile, while singling me out and offering up a panto-worthy performance. I think I was actually suffering from mild postnatal depression and the one thing someone in a dark fug doesn't require is enforced jazz hands. The internal tutting burst out into absolutely nothing, because I am British. But I never returned, because I needed to find sunshine on my own – starting with a ray here and there, building up to the full flood of light. But *sans* tambourine.

While I loved mate-whose-baby-slept-through-the-night, I also realised I needed some other folks around to sit in a hole with for a bit. When it comes to finding your maternal mates, it does not matter if you're into breast-feeding, bottle-feeding or Instagram-feeding, as long as you can look someone in the twitching peepers and feel less alone in the parenting minefield.

My biggest breakthrough in finding kindred maternal spirits was, in part, sparked by my dad's advice. He was a big advocate of class tunnel-vision. He said, 'Don't look up to people and don't look down on people – treat the Queen as you would the binman.' After a particularly rough day exchanging Pog cards at school, he also chirped up with, 'However close you are to someone, don't call them your "best friend" – it isolates others'; and 'Try and talk about things, not people.' I obviously ignored everything because I was a self-indulgent teenager at the time and believed in my own ways. Those ways were generally influenced by one-hit-wonder Hanson.

The eagle only landed when words like 'squad' and 'gang' started edging into my subconscious. What is this squad? Should I be in one? Does one require this athleisure clothing I've been hearing good things about? After a mild run-in – I was 100 metres away in the entrance of Poundland – with an actual gang in Northampton in 1996, I didn't want to really be in one of those. I still occasionally hold my keys between my index and middle finger as a weapon in the hope that I can poke someone into submission if trouble descends.

Either way, squad or gang, I realised within that first year of Mae's life that I had neither.

I was a floater.

I had a bunch of people I knew who definitely didn't want me to die.

There's the mate who chats about the grot stories on the *Daily Mail* sidebar of shame, the one who you've known for twenty-five years who knows about that snog from that-boy-whose-name-you-didn't-catch in 1995.

There's the mate from NCT.

The ones who you've met through vague social-media lurking and who start to feel like total keepers despite only meeting them twice.

One is a mate-of-a-mate who boldly WhatsApped me to ask if I fancied lunch (always a yes, regardless of the hour) and said, 'My best mate has just moved to New York, my other mama mates have moved out of London. I've been abandoned and you're, like, five minutes down the road. Will you be my friend?' Two weeks later I was closer to her than a Gillette Venus razor to an armpit.

Over the years I'd gathered a band of eclectic people who don't want me to cark it, like a friendship pick 'n' mix. But instead of the irksome 'you can't sit with us' blather of teenage years, in motherhood, anyone can sit anywhere. You can sit with us, them, the woman at Brixton Tube station playing Chumbawamba's 'Tubthumping' on her Pringle tin. Anyone who goes out of their way to exclude others is – as my mum would say – 'just being a bit silly, really'.

Don't make the mistake of thinking others have this elusive squad-gang-thang down because there's a photo of them with a few other mothers on the internet. The internet can make you feel like the loneliest, most-mammary-leaking mama on the planet, but it's really just one massive mosh pit of knack-ered souls holding on to the nearest gurning person.

My core team in the early days comprised a bunch of people I met everywhere from park benches to playgroups. I was, in many ways, a maternal vagrant. But this random bunch soon became a WhatsApp group that was the key to unlocking the sunshine in my mind.

The true breakthrough came when Mae started crawling. I was in the bedroom when I heard a faint whimpering from Douglas the beagle. I continued folding Mae's Babygros and ignored the canine sounds, assuming he just wanted to eat the contents of the bin again. The whimpering reached a crescendo and had a slightly different tone than usual. I am not sure my eyes were ready for the sight that lay ahead.

There was Mae, fingering Douglas' anus. Her tiny, pure little digits were probing his rectal arena.

The most disturbing realisation was that Douglas had not moved. He was lying there in what looked like a mixture of confusion and enjoyment. I did not know where to begin – break up this disturbing union, disinfect child, order child gate to separate them, never leave them alone together or exit the building.

I remember thinking I could cry at the dog-fingering situation that lay grimly before me or I could share this on our WhatsApp group and see if I was, in fact, a terrible mother.

A separate group was immediately set up by my friend Dita, entitled 'beagle rimming' and I laughed. I laughed a lot and a ray of light edged its way into my knackered mind. It wasn't the support group I'd imagined pre-baby, but it was support all the same and sometimes you've got to let go of those whimsical ideals in favour of a detailed analysis of the traumatic canine situation that sits before you.

And boy do you need that laughter on tap when work comes back into the parental equation. Your union of caring folk is needed even more as your partner – or you – exits the building to pull in a merry dime after those first two weeks when you're both on leave. Solo parenting brings its own peaks and troughs. Peaks? Seeing your kid properly gurn for the first time on the swings or sipping your first Aperol spritz at 2 p.m. on a Monday. Troughs? Running out of wet wipes in a wee-splattered public toilet, staring down at a faecal explosion and never feeling more alone.

I bore the brunt of solo parenting, as most mums do, though some companies are slowly waking up to the fact that dads might choose to parent, too. (Yep, they don't just spunk and leave, folks.) But whoever returns to work, remember it's okay on both sides not to feel chirpy 24-7.

Bedtime for me usually ran thus: Mae's refusal to go in the bath, her refusal to eat, her refusal to let me undress her or brush her tooth. But despite these tantrums, I always ended the night tucking her up in bed, whispering, 'You are brilliant, I love you and you can do anything you put your mind to.' I've said it when she couldn't hear me, and when she had thrown a faux IKEA cauliflower in my face. I couldn't say where it came from but I believe it's partly from my own mum – the woman who never had brakes on her rattly old Dutch bike.

It was 1989 and I was signed up to the skipping race at Leighton Buzzard's Linslade Lower School. It was one of those summers that seem to only happen when you were eight – parched grass, cobalt skies and a relentless flow of Mr Whippy. I was nervous, I didn't think I had it in me to beat Gillian Cartwheel (her actual name). Mum packed me an extra-special sandwich, cut into the shape of a Care Bear, and sent me off to sports day with the words, 'Focus on the finish line and forget the competition.'

I lost. I flopped to the ground after about five seconds, landing in a dusty heap on the floor as Gillian skipped to glory. I might not have won – in fact, if we call a spade a spade, I was a long way from that coveted rosette – but I believed I could win. My mum had instilled in me from an early age that it's not what everyone else is doing that matters but how you get yourself there that counts. In 1990 I cleaned up – winner of skipping, second in the sack race, and the beanbag and coit race was a no-brainer.

Without The Year of Shame (Gillian didn't let me forget it until she wanted an invite to my Alton Towers birthday party), I might not have had my triumphant comeback. So I think the big thing that held me together in those early days of motherhood when Matt was at work was making sure I uttered those words every day, regardless of what had happened. It was a routine that made me feel I was doing at least one thing right a day.

I also found it handy steering clear of social media in those first few months. For all its frothy coffees and perky peonies, the internet, specifically Instagram, is unashamedly a place of comparison. Seven years ago Matt and I had approximately nineteen nice people in our lives (now it's nine: we had to cull ten due to sheer exhaustion) against whom to compare ourselves. Now we're in a world where there are bucketloads (specifically 456 million active users on Instagram) of people out there with seemingly much better stuff/friends/babies/food/Scandi chic/ delicately ringed fingers/lives than us. In that first year with Mae, I sometimes felt like I was living in a comparative drug den, feeding her Dr Pepper from a shoe with only the faint buzz of the QVC channel in the background. Or so it felt.

The reality is that you've just spotted a pair of rogue undies under your bed or unearthed a soggy cucumber from the fridge – nothing dramatic, but with someone's powder-pink SMEG fridge beaming out of your phone, you can't help but wonder if they, too, have soggy cucumber disintegrating beneath the rucola. You invariably come to the conclusion that they don't, and that makes you sad as you dispose of the limp, stinking vegetable in your squeaky bin.

It's natural. Other than a few really good people like that guy on the news who saved a penguin, we're not by nature programmed to support people *all* the time.

'You get more explicit and implicit cues of people being happy, rich, and successful from a photo than from a status update,' says Hanna Krasnova of Humboldt University Berlin, co-author of *Envy on Facebook: A Hidden Threat To Users' Life Satisfaction*. 'A photo on Instagram can very powerfully provoke immediate social comparison, and that can trigger feelings of inferiority.'

We are a social media world of comparers. A multibillion-pound fashion industry revolves around us following 'influencers' and ensuring we're rocking that neon pom-pom hat with extendable ears – ensuring we're 'keeping up' with the trends.

Who hasn't seen a selfie on Instagram and scoured the background for clues about lifestyle? A wanton, bobbly sock in the background offers up some relief, whereas a pristine, cream carpet embellished with an unopened Whistles bag can cause subconscious alerts of 'need more stuff; distressed with current life choices'.

While there's nothing terrible about comparison – it's good

to know what's out there and it can be inspiring - it's not, from my experience, all sunshine and perfectly positioned roses when on maternity leave. It's not going to help you on that 4.13 a.m. breast-feed when your mammaries are leaking into your IKEA Önskedröm cushion and your undercarriage resembles a pack of Sellotaped-together bacon lardons.

When those photos flow in during the small hours as the fashion mavens waft about New York papping their lattes and you're slobbering into a bowl of Nescafé, it helps you to do one of two things: appreciate or unfollow.

Depending on my hormonal state, those two words saved me from a world of comparison and, perhaps, hints of depression in that first year. Because in a world of powder-pink SMEG fridges, it's important to bear in mind that sometimes those actually living life have a limp cucumber fermenting in the underbelly of their vegetable drawer.

Talking of phallic legumes, it was around this time that I started to get the right horn on again. Since having Mae, my sex drive had scarpered for the hills; like Gollum in *Lord of the Rings*, I cherished precious sleep far more than a quick fumble. After a fair amount of research (Googling), I realised this is not so unusual. According to a study on parents aged thirty-two to fifty-five by the *Times'* sex columnist, Suzi Godson, 44 per cent had sex weekly, 32 per cent had sex monthly, 11 per cent had sex annually, 9 per cent never have sex and 4 per cent had sex every day.

First, Suzi's job – what a divine occupation. Second, 4 per cent: who are you? Is it a lacklustre rummage under The White

Company sheets or a full-on twenty-eight-minute grot-fest with Agent Provocateur accoutrements? I'm sure Suzi has a wealth of PVC bounty hidden in her love den and enough worthy anecdotes to fuel a turbo hen do. There's no doubt she's 99 per cent a bona fide bonk oracle, but those 4 per cent immediately make me think I should be draped in black lace, peeling grapes on a velveteen chaise longue, awaiting my life lobster's return from work.

What those percentages don't account for is the variance of shag. Those vows state 'through good times and bad', but what they don't include is the ugly. Ugly, I'm-wearing-puppy-emblazoned-pjs-and-am-so-tired-I-could-conk-out sex counts. Sure, it's the romantic underdog, but much like the bargain bin in Tesco three minutes before closing time, bread is bread. And a girl's gotta eat – whether it's £1.34 Hovis or a thrifty 32p discount loaf.

My life on maternity leave was about soggy muslins, wet wipes, a strong lip and ugly sex. So chuck me those mashed-up fairy cakes and pop that dry Hovis thick-cut loaf in the basket; allow me to rummage through those perished floury baps in search of a rock-hard bloomer. Because sometimes when you delve into that bin, you can leave wondering why you don't shop there every day.

But then I read something that said: research has revealed that one in four British women feel stressed every single day, as opposed to just one in ten men.

So based on some possibly dodgy research, I realigned the OCD stars and let it all hang out. We're talking Lego gathered by the plughole of the bath and Babybels liberally scattered about the lounge after a CBeebies meltdown.

When the stress-induced eye twitch starts, just sit back, brace yourself, whack *Frozen* on (for the 147th time) and let it go.

It is here that we must put ketchup on the table. I can chart my student life with this trusty condiment: at 3 a.m., when everyone else had dispersed in a mashed-up haze, she was always there for me. United with vinegary red wine she delivered a stealth richness to my spag bol that no amount of Tesco Value purée could rival; she's always the last condiment standing in the fridge.

But after we embarked on Project Procreation she became a seemingly cruel mistress. With a sugar-crazed *enfant terrible* on my maternity leave watch, our relationship has become schizoid, vicious and unhealthy. If my friends truly knew what went down between us, they'd tell me to 'bin the bitch' and move on to a more wholesome condiment.

I reluctantly reach for her (E-numbers visibly IN MY FACE) when Mae is having a particularly vile fish-finger-related melt-down and everyone is crying. I craved her when I had thirteen minutes twenty-four seconds to get Mae to eat that painstak-ingly hand-prepared Ella's Kitchen sweet potato mash before the iPad crashed and I had to source the charger from 'the drawer of doom'. I even secretly slip her into things when my mum is around so it looks like I'm a great parent whose child is always ready to heartily chow down. ('Yeah, she seems to be eating fine with us at the moment.')

And then, when the last irksome mew of Igglepiggle is done and Mae is dreaming of a psychedelic Katie Morag scampering around the Cairngorms, I would vow to start the next day afresh. I would banish the ketchup to the back of the shelves, to the graveyard of condiments – behind the dusty Lea & Perrins, left of the jar of unnamed pickles from our Vietnamese honeymoon in 2010 – in the hope that the 'out of sight, out of mind' approach might work.

Who am I kidding? She's a saucy minx, she knows I'll return. She knows that in that first year you will eventually, inevitably succumb to everything you smugly promised would never happen on your watch. In many ways, these are the three pillars of early years parenting:

Dummy.
Ketchup.
iPad.

Papa Pukka.

One New Year's Eve, aged about seventeen, two friends and I were in a shabby London boozer and gave £20 to a burly man in a bomber jacket, hoping to get some ecstasy in return. Because we were scrawny halfwits with fewer street smarts than a barn owl, he never came back. But we went to our rave anyway (happy hardcore and jungle. I wore white gloves because I was cool*).

* I was not cool.

Those events didn't sell alcohol because the amphetamine-giddy crowd never used to buy any, and so we flung our limbs about like epileptics until 7 a.m., fuelled by nothing more than sugary drinks and cigarettes. We spent most of the long journey back to my friend's house in stomach-cramping fits of giggles, a strange kind of dopeyness across us. It was probably the first time any of us had been up for twenty-four hours without any chemical inducement, and we could barely operate a Travelcard between us, such was our slow-wittedness. It might have been the effect of nine hours listening to repetitive beats in a large shed on the Isle of Dogs, but I suspect that the lack of sleep had an impact too.

One 2010 study (in the snappily titled *International Journal of Occupational Medicine and Environmental Health*) found that twenty-four hours without sleep has a similar effect to having 0.10 per cent blood-alcohol content. That's higher than the drink-drive limit in every country that has one.

The researchers found that 'judgment is affected, memory is impaired, there is deterioration in decision making, and a decline in eye–hand coordination'. On top of that, 'you're more emotional, attention is decreased, hearing is impaired'.

By thirty-six hours, you are at a higher risk of a heart attack. At forty-eight hours, the body starts to shut down for 'micro-sleeps': spells of thirty seconds or so where the brain goes into a sleep state – the eyes remain open but essentially blind, as your mind stops processing information. By seventy-two hours, the hallucinations usually begin.

Of the many morally troubling techniques used at the US

facility in Guantánamo Bay, sleep deprivation was considered the most effective. Detainees were kept awake through 'use of repetitive loud noises', most famously by playing the Barney the Dinosaur music on repeat. CIA officials praised sleep deprivation for 'eroding prisoners' will to resist'.

All of the above may be things that new parents recognise. We might not be subject to it for such long periods, and newborns don't tend to waterboard people (projectile male weeing aside), but the cumulative effect of broken sleep can have similar results, especially if one partner – typically the mother – bears most of the burden. One study of more than 1,800 people (carried out by a mattress company, natch) reckons that new parents get an average of 5.1 hours sleep per night in the first year. That tots up to forty-four days of lost sleep over the year, based on the recommended average of eight hours per night. That's about one third of your year's kip.

You'll be knackered, is what I'm saying, and it's all very disorientating. When Mae called out in the night, I would wake up confused and grumpy, crashing about and stubbing my toe, bumping into an equally bleary-eyed Anna and generally not being too sure of who I was or what I did. For the first couple of weeks I was on paternity leave and able to reclaim some shut-eye during the day. But after a few months back at work, my eyes were sinking as fast as my spirit and I quietly cursed this blameless infant for thieving my sleep and sanity.

Part of the reason this is such an emotionally testing time is that the thing that interrupts your sleep is a sharp, loud noise that we have attuned to (over several millennia) as something impossible to ignore. Those tiny lungs can wail at a sharp 115 decibels. Around 90 decibels is considered what humans can listen to without feeling discomfort. One hundred and fifteen decibels is loud enough to cause damage to the inner ear after fifteen minutes, if you're close enough. It's a tiny bit quieter than a pneumatic drill, ambulance siren or really aggro ice-cream van, as demonstrated here:

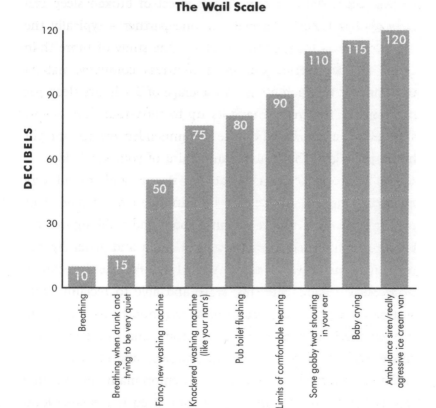

The Wail Scale

When they go, babies can really go. Mae's first summer in Amsterdam was suffocatingly hot. The city's position a few metres below sea level means that the summer air gets thick and humid, and the slow-moving canals bring armies of mosquitos. We had a small, second-floor apartment and kept the windows open and fans on full, but the air remained heavy. Mae was a few months old and Anna was having her first post-birth night out with friends. But the heat was too much for our little bug and she wailed at full bellow. I fed her, I changed her, I fanned her and cuddled her, but nothing made the noise stop. I rocked her back and forth in my arms and in her crib. I quietly sang 'Hush Little Baby' and 'Sweet Child O' Mine' (complete with *doo-doo doo-doo doo-doo doo-doo* opening guitar solo).

After about thirty minutes, I wondered if I could call an ambulance, just to have someone take her away for a moment so my brain could breathe. But she had no mozzy bites or rashes, no external signs of harm; she was just incredibly pissed off. After about forty-five minutes, I discovered that if I lifted her up, from my chest to above my head, something in that movement, whether the rushing breeze or the change of position, briefly calmed her. The noise stopped for a few blissful seconds, before starting again. So I did it again, like a standing shoulder press with a very delicate 3-kg weight. I did it every thirty seconds for about an hour, holding her over our bed in case my arms gave out. Each time she paused, I'd whisper 'there, there', or any other supposedly comforting noise. When my arms felt weak, I'd lay her down and stare dumbly at her while the noise continued, her face bright red and contorted in rage.

I put her in her crib and closed the door, but that agonising noise continued. It came through the walls and scratched around inside my skull. I found myself developing a new understanding of those tragic tales of broken-minded parents harming their infants. Then back to the shoulder press, the swaying, the cuddles and the shushing.

I kept telling myself that no child has ever cried for ever, and that the noise must eventually end. She finally drifted off a few minutes before Anna returned to find a man with bigger arms than when she left, and a mild case of post-traumatic stress disorder.

Over those first few months, neither of us slept for more than four continuous hours and Anna took the brunt of it. She was the food source and the one that Mae most wanted to nuzzle. When the wailing went off in the night, she was first to wake. Occasionally I'd be faking sleep to shirk my paternal responsibilities, but mostly I was so far under that it would take me longer to stir. Sometimes I'd get a grumpy prod to go and fetch our progeny, sometimes I would do it automatically, and at the very least I'd stir by the time Anna had returned to bed to feed.

They say that the maternal brain is more highly attuned to a baby's cry, and there has been some research to back that up, at least in rodents. A 2015 study published in the magazine *Nature* found that oxytocin, which surges in mothers after childbirth, changes the way sounds are processed in the brains of mice.

When virgin mice were given oxytocin, their behaviour in response to baby mice crying mimicked that of mothers. The dosed-up virgin mice began fetching the pups by the scruffs of their necks and returning them to the nest. The theory is that, at least in mice (because again, mice are not people), oxytocin turns up the volume of crying babies in the brains of mothers.

And there is also a little science to back up the oft-peddled male claim that 'I just didn't hear anything.' One study, covered in the journal *NeuroReport*, put eighteen men and women in a brain scanner and played the sound of a hungry baby crying. In the female brains, the sound interrupted 'awake resting' activity – the idle mulling that your mind does when nothing much is going on. The brains of men, regrettably, 'carried on without interruption', their brains perfectly happy to rest.

The burden could never by fifty/fifty, given that Anna had the milk, but I still wonder, looking back, if I did enough to even out the impact.

Your body adapts to some extent, and you get used to broken sleep, but it takes its toll. Our focus shifted to one task above all others – keeping the tiny human alive – but we also found ourselves in a dumb fug of 'coping', with Mae at about three months old and still waking three or four times a night.

I was moved by a strange sensation one night, awake but not, the greyness of half-sleep across my closed lids. I felt uneasy, but wasn't sure why. I was worried and felt needed, like Mae was in danger. I awoke to see Anna at the end of our bed, asleep but upright, dutifully swaddling my right foot.

I'd found returning to work after two weeks to be a sweet relief. I was freelance and needed to be earning money, and returning to an office gave me a break from the monotony of changes and feeds and allowed me, for eight blissful hours, to be a functioning adult, free of the tinkling of baby mobiles and the smell of milky turds. As the one going to work every day, I had also been given a fairly easy run on the night shifts. I might do the change after Anna had done the feed, or do the burping so she could feed and then go straight back to sleep, but she was taking most of the burden. But Dutch maternity leave only runs to three months and with Anna's return to work looming (more on that in Chapter 8), we found an idyllic nursery called the Witte Vlinder (white butterfly) in the bottom two floors of a converted townhouse. They had about fifty kids from a dozen countries and a squad of young, smiling Dutch women who looked after them.

With Anna due to return to work four days a week, I adjusted my week to give me what the Dutch call a *papadag* (or 'daddy day'): I'd work from 7:30 a.m. to 7 p.m. for four days, with every Wednesday off to look after Mae. Partly this was down to understanding clients and partly it was because I said 'no' when people demanded things outside these hours.

Three days of day-care a week cost us about €1,200 a month. This was an issue, as I didn't remember having a spare €1,200 a month before becoming a parent and I'm still not sure how we covered it and still managed to eat. Anna's salary for four days a week meant she might be taking home a few hundred euros a month after day-care costs.

But we really didn't have much choice. She'd worked furiously hard over two years to find a company in Amsterdam where she could do something that met her experience level, that she enjoyed, and where limited Dutch language skills didn't make a difference. If she gave it up, she might not find another suitable job in the city. So we paid strangers to guard our infant. Anna spent her last days of maternity leave sitting at the Witte Vlinder with Mae, making sure she was happy. They played with the kids and fed them well, before putting them to sleep for regular naps in cots stacked four-high, like cages at a vet. But the atmosphere was good and the kids seemed happy, so that's what we did.

The next Monday, I made the first deposit. I strapped Mae to my chest and stepped on the tram like any other commuter, but one carrying, instead of a briefcase, a tiny version of themselves. I wondered how it might feel to leave someone so small and fragile and vulnerable in the care of strangers. Whatever the financial demands and the need to continue life after a nipper, I wondered if she would be happy once left behind – if they'd know what her different cries meant and if they'd be quick to respond. I wondered if this was the right thing to do.

I handed Mae over to a young woman called Shannon, who had about the purest and most naturally friendly spirit I have ever witnessed in another human being. She beamed and cuddled our little parcel, who immediately nuzzled into her. And so I left to go to work, with the faint mix of guilt and relief that I think most parents feel. The guilt came from worrying that she was too young or might feel abandoned, but the relief came from being off parental duty and handing the responsibility over to someone else.

And this was the odd conflict I found with being a parent. I found that whenever I cared for her, I couldn't wait for Mae to be silently napping, but after ten minutes or so I'd want her to wake up so I could pull peculiar faces at her and sniff her soft head. My feelings with day-care were similar. I wanted to clock off for the relative calm of going to work, but at various points in the day I felt a sudden longing to see her and feel her weight in my arms. It's a mix of feelings that has never left. There are times when I want silence – to know she is sleeping or being cared for by someone else. But then I'll be on the Tube or in a meeting or tapping away at my desk and feel a surge in my chest, like extra air has been pumped into my lungs. I will immediately want to know where she is and feel a strong urge to be there or have her with me, wriggling in my arms or dangling over my shoulder: to hear her giggle and know that I had caused it.

Schedule or snuggle?

We'd been sustained by new-parent euphoria for the first few months, but months three to six became a steady slog. With us both working, that cumulative lack of sleep was making us ratty and the tiredness began to hit us physically. My concentration would drift, and Anna and I became impatient with each other. Getting Mae to sleep through the night became the most important thing in our lives and Anna would sometimes cry from tiredness. We became obsessed with methods and techniques.

These basically boil down to two camps: schedulers, who have a fixed routine of feeding and napping, regardless of what baby wants (though you can only start doing this after a couple of months), and snugglers, who feed and nap their baby according to its own whims and wails (known as 'infant-led'). We landed in the former camp, following *The Contented Little Baby Book* by Gina Ford. It's a script that some like and others hate, breaking your day into little chunks and also directing you to eat and sleep to a schedule. It involves waking your baby to feed it and deliberately not making eye contact during feeds before naps. It can feel counter-intuitive but for us, it worked. Others think it's a little mean and find that their baby doesn't work that way: that, with enough hugs, the bambino will eventually go through the night of its own accord.

There has been surprisingly little research into what works best. One 2006 study (called *Hugger v Scheduler*) broadly found that scheduled babies slept for longer, sooner (often five-hour stretches at night), but that they grizzled more too (121 minutes in every 24 hours, compared with 82 minutes for the cuddled ones). And there is very little evidence of what the effects are in later childhood.

My only advice is to do what works best for you and yours.

But whatever route you choose, there was one piece of kit that became invaluable to us: the 'miracle blanket'. There are a few brands around, but once we shifted from a plain muslin to one of these for swaddling, sleep came much more easily. You just wrap your nipper up like a spring roll, so that they feel calm and secure.

8

Working it out

Mother Pukka.

As maternity leave came to an abrupt halt, I went back to the nine-to-five hamster wheel of doom. Overweight, over-exhausted, overrun with guilt, and a bit over it all before it had begun. I returned to work at the fashion label SuperTrash and suddenly felt like a fish out of fashionable water in my stretch 'jeggings' and tapered tops to hide the 'gunt' (gut and 'c' word rhyming with runt) that had emerged post-splashdown. I felt more Trashbag than SuperTrash.

Every day in that first month back, I joined the dots on my knackered face with foundation and kept chuntering on, hoping it would get easier. And it did eventually. I started to appreciate a wee without a nipper wailing mid-flow; coffee breaks felt like a veritable mini-break despite pining for Mae like a salivating Douglas might pine for the last chip in the world.

Every day I pitched up to that office I could feel fragments of my mind realigning. I started to enjoy work and the Dutch truly had the right approach to work–life balance, with my boss even saying, at 5.02 p.m., 'Why are you still here? Go and enjoy the kid.'

Just as I was finding my feet, Matt got offered a job in the UK and we were set to return to Blighty, our homeland – somewhere that felt quite foreign after eight years away. A massive life shift was again on the cards and we battened down the hatches as a family to navigate three stressful familial trials in one fell swoop: house move, new(ish) baby and new job. Well done us and our life choices.

I bagged a job, while Matt worked all hours of the day at a travel website. It was at that time that my mum stepped in to help and save us the costs of a couple of days' nursery each week, and I realised the Dutch approach to work–life balance was worlds apart from the UK.

I struggle with the terms 'working mother' or 'stay-at-home mum' as much as I have a problem with 'single', 'married' and anything else that requires a box to be ticked. I do, however, believe in doing my duty as a parent. We're all essentially just trying to keep fish fingers on the table and *PAW Patrol* on the TV.

But there was one evening after work when I failed to pick my daughter up from nursery at 6 p.m. I landed in a sweaty, mangled maternal heap at 6.13 p.m., apologising profusely and uttering excuses ('Tube, meeting, leaves on line, battery died, chewing gum on shoe'), to the matronly response from the duty manager of: 'It's not ideal.'

It flipped a switch. I took out all my frustration about this inflexible, expensive day-care system on this poor woman, who was simply a cog in a hulking great machine – a system that left me earning approximately £3 an hour after day-care costs were paid. In Amsterdam, I was actively encouraged to reduce my hours to accommodate my family life. In the UK, 'flexibility' felt like a dirty word. It's a system that's priced nearly half a million British mothers out of work according to think-tank IPPR, and it's a system that leaves parents frazzled and shouting at those who are there to help.

It's not ideal at all. This woman, who kept my child safe for forty hours a week, couldn't have put it better. It broke my heart explaining to my daughter every morning why Mama had to go to work rather than play with the 'cayons' (crayons). Hearing 'Mama's here! Mama's here!' when I was just three minutes late to pick her up – because some half-wit managed to get his briefcase trapped in a Tube door – and she was the last one left, ate me up. Seeing her sitting there, alone but for her treasured little 'Peppy' (Peppa Pig) rucksack and some primary-hued creation in hand is a sight that could render me broken.

So, I was all too aware it wasn't ideal. I knew those thirteen minutes were less than ideal because they were the longest minutes of my day. All I wanted was a system that offered some leeway, some flexibility, some financial relief to those who want to – or have to – work. Or at the very least, that challenges businesses to eschew Dolly Parton's 'working nine to five' mantra – when did it slip to 6 p.m.? – and not leave mothers (or fathers) edging out of the office, feeling like pariahs.

There's no ideal working situation as a mother, it's all down to circumstance, necessity and doing everything you can to keep everyone under your wing alive and well. But for me, that first year of working on UK soil left me with little choice but to quit while I was behind.

At school I never got the prize for 'excellence', always 'effort'. I'm a grafter, a reviser, a Post-it note lover, a Sellotape-over-the-cracks kinda gal who has one USP (other than Grade 3 on the triangle): determination.

That grit had seen me move from my *Practical Caravan* days to senior copywriter in the glossier realms of L'Oreal – a job I'd wanted since I first learnt how to use a lash-boosting double-ended mascara.

So quitting hurt. It was against everything I'd grown to know about myself. As women, mothers, wives, partners and friends, we don't quit. We fail repeatedly at things, we mess up, we stress out, but we never throw in the towel – however much Weetabix is being mashed into our faces by an E-number-fuelled toddler.

But I had to quit a career that stemmed from reading teen rag *Bliss Magazine* in 1991 and thinking, 'I like words, I want to write some of those, this can be my thing!'

It led to an internship at *Heat Magazine* where I met H from Steps (a career high); I then bagged a job as a reporter on *Practical Caravan* (is there ever an impractical caravan?) and ended up being their tow-bar expert before slipping onto *Horticulture Week* and learning how to spell 'fuchsia'.

It was a career that led me to Matt – a fellow reporter on

the salubrious *Human Resources* magazine, and took me to Dubai, a Swarovski-encrusted dictatorship where I wrote about shoes and handbags for *Grazia*; then onto Amsterdam where I was the vice editor at *Time Out* – I would pitch up to sex parties and write notes, before interviewing the founders on their favoured lube.

That's just my (fairly low-brow) career path; every mother, every parent has one. We all make decisions along the way – from seemingly essential GCSE choices and summer pub jobs to careers and ultimately deciding how to make everything you've worked for work with your family.

I'm friends with baristas, barristers, stay-at-office mums, stay-at-home mums, Instamums, Instabums, bloggers, sloggers, mum bosses and mum-don't-give-a-tosses, cupcake bakers, cake fakers and everything in between. But the one thing that unites us all as parents is the struggle to make work actually work.

I don't think it does. I gave it a good innings but at thirty-four I had to hang up my press pass and gracefully edge out of the office, because I didn't want to be the one scrambling like a rasping Labrador to day-care any more.

I couldn't see Mae, at 6.13 p.m., sat alone and wondering why everyone else has been picked up. I couldn't turn my back on her any longer as she hollered 'Mama' and begged for me to stay in the morning. During the week, she was with her carers for forty hours and awake with us for sixteen: that ratio cut deep. I didn't want to have to shell out a quid for every minute past 6 p.m. I arrived at nursery. And I couldn't skulk out of the office at 5 p.m., feeling like a massive slacker.

I couldn't do it. And I know I'm not alone – 54,000 mothers feel pushed to leave employment every year, according to the Equality and Human Rights Commission (EHRC).

And this covers the full gamut – those who are forced out by bell-end bosses (one friend said her company only ever discussed her 'leaving', never going on 'maternity leave' when she announced her pregnancy) to those who trot out of the office merrily only to regret it six months later (it's hard to go back, there's always someone bouncier and less yoghurt-stained ready to slot into your position).

And what hurts more is that the L'Oreal Group, a huge multibillion-pound company employing more than 78,600 people, was great. It's one of the best companies I've worked for – the people are great, the work is great, the double-ended volume mascara is great. I wish I'd had a dramatic exit with flouncing and an official escorting me out of the building as I hollered, 'You're not worth it.'

They gave me as much flexibility as the role could muster, but they moved our creative studio a further ninety minutes away from us (I saw Mae one hour a day as it was) and that one change was the straw that broke this mama's back. The role was flexible, but not Cirque du Soleil level – I needed a glitter-embellished contortionist as an employer to make this kind of role work.

But what gave me hope as I quit my honest-to-god dream job is the wave of parents rolling up their Sudocrem-smattered sleeves going, 'Let's do this.' A bunch of people who have realised big brands aren't getting it and probably won't in our lifetime. For every fresh company that offers flexible working for people – we're not just talking parents, but everyone – there's 7,690 that are set in their archaic ways.

What I've seen in this brave new digitally savvy parental world is that with some hard graft, an understanding of social media and enough people willing to lift up instead of tear down, we can do this.

We're just a rabble of parents who don't want it all, but want something. My something was to be with my daughter and pull in cold, hard cash whenever, wherever I could (without being illegal) – be that in the playground or at my ketchup-smattered kitchen table.

Career, you were fruitful but I had to stumble (not jump – too knackered) into something else – something that involved fighting for flexible working in global brands; fighting to reduce extortionate day-care rates and trying to build a platform that champions parent-run businesses one Instagram post at a time.

I quit my job because it was time to see what else was out there – even if that was just having Play-Doh embedded into the carpet. Or, perhaps, having no money.

As with any parental decision, leaving my job was one loaded with eye-twitching worry – the largest concern being cash and how to get it without a multibillion-pound beauty empire behind me, and how to keep it coming in steadily enough to replace my dissolving Topshop dungarees and stay housed.

While I don't want to dampen spirits (mainly my own), no

choice is perfect. As parents, worry is embedded in our DNA. My worries are, perhaps, larger now than when I was galloping with a sweat-on to day-care from L'Oreal HQ. And like everything related to the little person whose Eskimo kisses and sleepy hand-squeezes light up your frickin' soul, sometimes we overthink it.

There is no perfect reality. Running your own business means you're working harder than you worked in the shackles of the nine-to-five. Dinnertime becomes punctuated with 'urgent emails', and working from the playground can lead to grazed knees and swings in faces. And that's particularly true of any business that relies on social media. I've seen parents setting up businesses – kid's clothes, teething necklaces, consultancies, achingly cool nappy bags and even a brilliant sock puppet company – working harder than they ever did in the nine-to-five. The minute their brood has been read the fast-track (skipping out the fox and snake) *Gruffalo*, and is peacefully snoozing, they're onto their Gmail like a rat out of an aqueduct.

You're wide-eyed and staring at a list of things to do – most of which won't translate to paying the mortgage because to have something to sell you must 'build the brand'. Build and they will come! But stacking up those social media bricks takes graft; it involves hair loss, marital discord, peaks, troughs, wearing the same Petits Filou-stained jumper three days in a row because you need to build instead of wash.

The reason I fight like a dog with a bone for flexible working is because setting up your own business (the seemingly wondrous and only alternative) is not parental Mecca. It's brilliant in so many ways – mainly control over when you eat a Hula Hoop multipack in one sitting (not office behaviour) – but it's certainly not the easy way out. There is no easy way out.

When you're the boss, there's no stationery cupboard, and when your computer crashes there's no Bob in IT to allay your fears that you've broken the internet (in a non-brand-building way).

But we are fuelled by a primitive maternal instinct that this will not fail. It can't. I am a mother and I have mouths to feed. I am a mother and I need to work around my family. I am a mother and I need to show my children that mothers can make shit happen too. I am a mother and I want you, Squidge, to be proud of me.

There's an undeniable pride in 'going it alone'. But for all the brilliance of building something yourself, there's a period of two to three years (perhaps more) where you might be rifling around in that Asda bargain bin praying for a 12p Hovis loaf. Success certainly doesn't come overnight, regardless of how it seems through the pixels.

So if you love the job you have now, fight for it. Make it work for you – push the flexible working boundaries. Be the one who brings the government's Working Forward pledge to your HR director and pave the way for others in your company to continue on their chosen career path.

If you choose to stay at home with your kids, don't feel the pressure to set something up just because everyone else on the internet seems to be doing so – own motherhood. It's a choice I would give my last Curly Wurly for. The stay-at-home versus go-to-work debate is as dated as Simon Cowell's elasticated waistline. Neither is better, both are valid.

And if you're thinking of setting something up, know that for all the dancing-lady-emoji joy it brings, you will go through a significant period of time when you feel a bit unhinged and when, hungry in central London, you try to buy a cheese-pickle sarnie and your card – and pride – gets declined.

I wish I could paint a more von Trapp picture of us self-employed folk frolicking in flexible-working paradise with money fluttering from the trees. But the hills aren't always alive and if you get to enjoy the occasional sunset – even if it is graffittied onto a wall – then perhaps that's actually enough. Perhaps that's my perfect something in a world that's telling me to have it all.

Papa Pukka.

I wasn't really ready to go home to England, and I wasn't really ready to leave Amsterdam. I liked the fact that in the mornings I would strap Mae to the front of my bicycle to take her to day-care, riding along leafy seventeenth-century canals, through streets so idyllic they looked like something from an estate agent's rendering, complete with smiling blonde women and preppy guys with sweaters over their shoulders. I liked that I could do that in under five minutes and set myself a working week of 7.30 a.m. to 7 p.m., four days a week, the fifth to be spent with my daughter. And I liked that this wasn't unusual in a country where many fathers had a 'daddy day' – one working day every fortnight to spend with your kids – written into their contracts. I liked our friends and our lives and my work.

But still there was the call of home. Anna had grown up in a small village and our sudden move abroad eight years before had curtailed her London adventure. I'd grown up in the city and always expected to move home one day.

Mae's limited vocabulary had more Dutch words than English, and while she could eventually be fluent in both, I had an odd need for her to be culturally British even though I didn't really know what that meant. On the simplest, most puerile level, I wanted her to know when people were taking the piss out of her in the British style and be sharp-witted enough to do the same in return.

Basically, I think we moved back so our daughter might one day have 'top bantz' and I'm not sure how that reflects on my parenting. (It reflects badly.)

So a job came up and we were gone. Having left the UK eight years earlier as a couple of barely three months' standing, we were back as working parents with a toddler.*

---

* You may be wondering what happened to Douglas, our flatulent beagle who once accidentally took heroin (see Chapter 1). As Mae started to walk, Doug's food obsession became a little dangerous. While he was incapable of intentionally hurting anyone (other than with his noxious gases), if given an opportunity he would try to steal Mae's food,

Over the next few months I became very aware of what we'd given up. We were both working long hours, and travelling for a combined two and half hours a day. Three days of day-care a week cost as much as our rent. Anna's parents swept in for the other two, collecting Mae from one of us amid the muddle of commuters at Shepherd's Bush station at 8 a.m. on a Tuesday morning, taking her on a ninety-minute journey to their house, then depositing her back at the same station at 6 p.m. on a Thursday. She was becoming like a boomeranging special delivery, and along with the guilt at handing her over like an Amazon return and the quiet longing while she was away was the awareness that without the help of Anna's folks I'm not sure how we would have made things work. On those evenings when Mae was away, we didn't have date nights or spend quality time together; we each worked late to make up for leaving 'early' at 5 p.m. one or two nights a week. But, we thought, this is how it is for parents.

And then, we thought, 'Does it have to be?' After a couple of months Anna started Mother Pukka. In the few hours left between sleeping, working and parenting, she effectively took on another job. She wanted to create something that spoke to others in similar predicaments, to offer empathy, entertainment and even occasionally some advice.

---

plucking biscuits from her toddler mitts, jumping up at her high chair and causing worrying wobbles. And once, in a park, plucking an ice cream from the hand of a passing five-year-old. We put him up for adoption and he went to live with a Dutch farmer as a companion for an elderly female beagle called Mabel.

It became a little bit of an obsession, and I was mostly a bystander. She built a website, then a following, and she did it while working full time and doing all the other things she always does – including about 60 per cent of the parenting and housework.*

So she did all these things while still being a committed friend to her buddies, still seeing the possibilities that lay ahead. And as it grew, alongside the silly puns and personal revelations, she began to bang a drum for flexible working.

It was probably the most stressful time we've had together. My working environment was difficult and the hours were long. Anna was effectively doing two jobs, and discovered that little bits of hair came out in the shower as the pressures began to build. Neither of us felt we were being particularly good parents.

We went on like that for a year and managed, just about, to buy a home. We had saved up some money in Amsterdam and with some help from Anna's parents and grandparents that deposit went from being enough to get a mortgage on a

---

* I've always done my bit domestically, but Anna's always done a bit more. We've never really discussed the divide but have gently taken up certain jobs, based primarily on what annoys each of us most. My own threshold for filth is a little higher, so I'm happy leaving a scaly shower or ignoring the weird mark on the hallway wall. The flipside is that I do the tax returns and the bills and suspect Anna's only turned on the washing machine twice in our time together, primarily because I would rather flay off my own kneecaps than go into a shop and buy new clothes, so have to 'do washes' on my limited wardrobe (and her extensive one) at a rate that would have Cinderella calling the scullery maids' union.

small flat in East London to one on a small house. It had no gas, no central heating, a fully functioning outdoor toilet and plaster that came off with the wallpaper. There was a lean-to that appeared to be made from papier mâché and the unheated kitchen was so cold that in the winter you could see your breath. It had a moth's nest and mice beneath the floorboards.

Within a week of signing the deeds, two things happened – I left my job to go freelance, and Anna quit hers to go full time with Mother Pukka. She'd worked for ten years to get to a stage at last where she earned a grown-up wage and a big-sounding job title. But she'd reached that stage while also being a mother and the two would not go together. So after three months she realised she had to quit.

And we decided that, alongside the goofy videos and cheesy puns, we would bang the drum for flexible working, and bang it louder and louder, so that by the time Mae is at the same stage of her working life, she has a few more options. It has seen us dance in Lycra-clad flash-mobs in town centres across the country. It has seen Anna lobby politicians in parliament and city halls. And, we hope, it will continue for as long as we can make it. Flexible working does not pit workers against bosses: it helps employers make more money and it helps staff live better lives. Here is why.

The Flexifesto: why businesses should do it

Too many of Britain's employers are unimaginative, overly cautious and unwilling to think beyond the nine-to-five.

This is something that blights almost everyone who works, but it blights parents more than most. Nearly nine million UK workers say they want to work flexibly but don't have the option.

And that's despite the fact that, since 2014, every employee in the UK with more than six months in their job has had the right to request flexible working. The trouble is that most who make the request are treated like toddlers demanding marzipan at bedtime.

But that attitude is an odd kind of self-harm: in most cases, flexible working means happier staff, lower costs and greater productivity. It's good for people and it's good for business.

Of course, there are some jobs where flexibility is harder to manage. No one wants all their town-centre coppers taking Friday nights off; call centres need heads attached to headsets at the hours people are most likely to call; you tend to need more firefighters on Guy Fawkes Night.

But in most roles that involve sitting at a desk (and that's a good 80 per cent of them in the UK), it makes no odds whether you write your report at 6 a.m., lunchtime, or midnight.

And even in those jobs that demand rapid responses, it rarely makes any difference whether you send that response from your sofa, or perched in front of your assigned piece of laminated MDF.

But it can make a lot of difference to you. In the UK, average commuting times are forty-six minutes a day, which is higher than anywhere else in the OECD (Organisation for Economic Co-operation and Development). In London, it's fifty-six minutes.

And once there, UK staff work longer hours than the French, the Germans, the Scandinavians and the Dutch, but are less productive than all of them.

Flexible working doesn't mean working less or slacking off; it means finding hours that suit your life and how you best work. If that happens to be sitting below strip lighting, so be it. But if you're most productive working from bed/a park/the local library, employers should have the imagination to allow that to happen.

And it's not just an issue for parents, either. It applies just as much to first-jobbers who nurse hangovers every Monday morning as it does to dads who like to do the school run.

And it isn't just a cuddly human issue: it's good economic sense. When parents drop out of work, the economy loses their knowledge and their tax revenue. And it's one of the few issues that both the unionists of the TUC and the employers at the CBI agree on: flexible working is better for staff, and it's better for profits.

The only people resisting are those who actually stand to benefit: employers themselves.

That resistance is, I think, driven by fear that people will slack off. Some will. If they do, give them a warning. If they continue to, then pull them back to their desk or give them the boot. But at least give them the option.

If employers are willing to offer it, my guess is that (with most parents at least) they can only win. So what's the business case?

SAVE RENT

For most businesses, the two main costs are people and property. Flexible working lets employers lower the latter. Lambeth Council claims it will save £4.5 million per year in property running costs by making sure that no more than 60 per cent of its staff are in at one time.

ATTRACT TALENT

Some 30 per cent of the UK's working population (8.7 million people) want flexible working but don't have it, yet only 6 per cent of advertised jobs with a salary above £20,000 actually offer it. If you're a firm with the imagination to offer it, you are immediately at a competitive advantage.

RETAIN TALENT

It costs more than £5,000 to hire a new employee in the UK. When you add costs associated with getting the newbie up to speed, that can exceed £30,000, arbitration service Acas recently reported, and more than £35,000 according to analysts Cebr. In its 2012 study, HR institute the CIPD found that 76 per cent of employers saw staff retention improve when they offered flexible working.

IMPROVE PRODUCTIVITY

This argument has become as undeniable as the case for the earth being round: 81 per cent of senior managers believe flexible working improves productivity. Three in five people who work flexibly put in more hours as a result of being allowed to do so. Another report found that 72 per cent of businesses reported increased productivity as a direct result of flexible working.

I want your flex: asking for flexible working

The reasons for denying flexible working tend to be knee-jerk and well rehearsed: 'If we did it for you, we'd have to do it for everyone', they might say, or 'How would I know you were doing any work?' Employers can decline your request for anything they consider to be a 'legitimate business reason'.

But there are answers for most of those, because in most cases flexible working makes good sense for businesses and their staff.

So we asked thousands of Instagrammers for the most common reasons why their requests for flexible working were turned down. There were some depressingly familiar trends, so we've listed them here, along with the arguments to make in return.

Option A is the sensible one, based on interviews with HR consultants and the very helpful people at Working Families. Option B is stat-tastic and straight to the point, while Option C is a little bolshie and may get you fired. The Cs came from me.

If you're at home, how will we know what you're doing?

A: By seeing what I do. I can take the time to report in more, I can suggest measurable objectives. Whatever it takes to make this work.

B: Perhaps you don't need to, and could focus on what I produce. One recent Stanford University study found that home-workers in China did 13.5 per cent more work than those in the office – that's almost a whole extra day's work each week – and were happier in their jobs.

C: The same way you do when I'm shackled to my laminated MDF desk/factory line/headset – by seeing how many spreadsheets/widgets/sales I've produced, you binary-thinking progress-obstacle.

It's too expensive.

A: It shouldn't mean more expense. I can suggest the hours in a way that works for both of us and it'll mean I'm happier and more loyal as a result.

B: Actually, it can save money. It costs on average £5,000 to hire a new employee in the UK. When you add the time costs of getting them up to speed, it hits £30,000, according to Acas. But 76 per cent of employers saw staff retention improve when they offered flexible working.

C: It'll cost you more to replace me. Now shuffle your tuckus over here and sign it off.

If we did it for you, we'd have to do it for everyone.

A: The business case is different each time and you're under no obligation to give it to everyone. In my case, I sufficiently want flexible working to succeed to make sure it does.

B: Great, you'll become a much more attractive employer.

Some 30 per cent of the UK's working population (8.7 million people) wants flexible working but doesn't have it, yet only 6 per cent of advertised jobs with a salary above £20,000 actually offer it.

C: Good. You'll have a happier workforce and earn more money. Now fetch your diary.

It's too difficult to manage.

A: I believe in two-way flexibility, and will do all I can to manage this myself. So trust me and at least let's have a go.

B: It can lead to management efficiencies, effectively keeping the business open for longer each day. There is lots of free advice and software online. And it's a lot easier to manage a company with great staff retention. In the US, for example, 46 per cent of companies that allow remote working say it has reduced attrition and 95 per cent of employers say it has a high impact on employee retention.

C: Not for anyone who can be trusted to operate a stapler it isn't. It isn't hard, is what I'm saying.

We have a shift system.

A: I'm asking to change my shift pattern, not end it. Why don't we explore with the whole team what is possible? I've already spoken to some of them and think we can come up with a rota that works. Why don't we have a trial period and review it?

B: Perhaps that is something that should be addressed. It is widely accepted that shift work reduces sleep quality, increases fatigue, anxiety, depression, neuroticism, adverse cardiovascular effects, gastrointestinal disorders and can be harmful to pregnant women.

C: Then shift it.

You'll be less productive.

A: I think the reverse is true. I want this to work, so will make sure that my productivity doesn't suffer.

B: In a survey of 2,200 businesses in the UK, 81 per cent of senior managers said flexible working improves productivity. A global survey of 20,000 business found that 72 per cent of businesses reported increased productivity as a direct result of flexible working.

C: You know what makes me unproductive? Not seeing my kid. Why not see what I can do when my mind's really on the job.

We have lots of impromptu meetings and need you here for those.

A: We can agree core hours when I'd be here, like 10 a.m. to 4 p.m. I'm not just going to hole up at home, and perhaps we'd be more productive with more scheduled meetings, so everyone can manage their time.

B: Remote meetings are more productive, because everyone gets to the point. They are greener, as they involve less travel.

Remote working is incredibly popular: a recent US survey found that 36 per cent of staff would choose it over a pay rise. And if you roll this out across the firm, you can save on rent, too. Lambeth Council will save £4.5 million per year in property costs by having no more than 60 per cent of its staff in at one time.

C: Can you spell 'Skype'? Would you like me to explain what telephones are?

Your rights

In the UK, since 2014, anyone with more than twenty-six weeks in their job has a right to request flexible working. Just put it in writing, explaining exactly what change you'd like and when, then date it and give it to your boss or HR folk. Follow up with a meeting request, just to help focus their minds. If you're anticipating bother, you might want to have a colleague present (though employers don't have to allow this). The big chiefs then have three months to settle things, including time for appeals. Legally, they're obliged to consider your request, but not grant it. They can turn it down for anything they consider a legitimate business reason. If they say no, you can appeal through your firm's usual procedure, whether that's a quiet chat or something more formal. If you're still not happy, you can turn to Acas, the arbitration organisation.

Types of flex

There are no limitations to what you can request. If you can prove that you'll get your work done and that it won't adversely affect others, you could ask to work a sixteen-hour day peppered with five-minute micro naps, or to do your contracted thirty-six hours in one fell swoop (unwise). These are more common:

HOME WORKING: Most aspects of traditionally office-based jobs can be done from anywhere with wi-fi, and employers are beginning to understand this. Just over half of the 32,000 employees quizzed for the 2015 Healthiest Company survey said they could sometimes work from home. To help make your case, you might want to agree to be in the office for certain 'core hours' like 10 a.m. to 4 p.m., or for a full day on Monday and Tuesday if those tend to be full of meetings, then do the rest at a time to suit you.

FLEXITIME: If they insist on having your bum on a seat all week, you can still ask for some flexibility around when that happens. Flexitime means that the traditional nine-to-five-period shifts to accommodate your life. If your nipper is in a play at 4 p.m., start work at 7 a.m. and leave early. This is one way that the card-punching mentality can help you to prove you're leaving early but still doing your bit.

JOB SHARING: One job split between two people, often working six days a week with one day of crossover. The main advantage for employers is that they get two brains for the price of one (and a bit), so twice the ideas, twice the energy, and a dedication to making these rarely available opportunities work out.

COMPRESSED HOURS: The average working week in the UK is forty-three and half hours (compared to forty hours for our more productive European neighbours). That works out as five days of working from 9 a.m. to 6.10 p.m. with a half-hour lunch. But it could as easily be done by working from 9 a.m. to 8.30 p.m. over four days (and still having time for lunch), with the fifth day spent caring for a child, parent or your golf swing.

Your rights after getting flex

Once you've done the hard part, there's the aftermath. According to the EHRC, a narrow majority of women who make flexible working requests have them approved. But 51 per cent of those women found that it had a negative impact on their career, with fewer work opportunities or negative comments from colleagues. More than a third failed to ask for the hours they really wanted through fear of negative consequences.

Your place might be fine, or you might face a little bit of snark. But then a little bit of snark seems to be inevitable wherever humans gather so don't let that put you off. Your workplace rights are not affected by working flexibly.

But the first stage is to ask. And the more folk who do that, the more normal it will become. Every year, awareness is growing, so why not be the one to increase it at your place. If you'd like to know more, these are good places to start:

Advice for staff on their rights and making the case:
workingfamilies.org.uk
acas.org.uk
citizensadvice.org.uk

Advice for employers on how flex can help productivity and profits:
cbi.org.uk
cipd.co.uk

9

Look who's walking

Mother Pukka.

My parental agenda is painfully simple: let her choose. For all the dinosaurs, princesses, blue and pink divides of the 1980s, just let the little nipper pick her lane. Then give her the space to change her mind every day, every minute or every second if she fancies.

Because, as women, we're not always a pretty shade of pink, and, as men, we're not always into the blue; sometimes we like a diplodocus and other days it's a Swarovski-encrusted pastel-hued crown. We're beyond all that archaic pigeonholing.

And that's where the 'C' word enters, despite its mildly naff connotations: confidence. There she is. There is absolutely no way of bringing up this word without glossy magazine covers spouting 'ten confidence-boosting tips' or worse into my grey matter. It's been cursed with the media wand of naffness and subsequently it's a sad, sorry collection of letters that no one wants to use. But it's at the heart of everything I focused (and focus) my parental efforts on when it comes to Mae. Confidence is the clunky old key that opens up all those doors of possibility – walking, talking, aspiring to be a 'sandwich maker' (Mae's current career goal). Without it, she's left with a worn piece of sandpaper and the promise of great things on the other side of that heavy oaken door: 'Just sand away poppet and you *might* get through!'

From those first wobbly steps and that moment when she said 'mama' (it was probably 'llama', her favourite animal, but I banked it all the same), confidence has been at the heart of everything I want Mae to hold close as she grows into a wonderful woman. A woman who will never think about sniffing poppers and will only edge into boyfriend territory aged twenty-one, when she's fully qualified to sort the keepers from the twats.

But how do you 'teach' confidence? It's not exactly on a par with the old ABCs, and where the hell is *Sesame Street* on all this? Big Bird – it's time to stop flapping and fly, my feathery friend.

One day I gave up on 'Wind the Bobbin Up' and asked Mae if she'd like to sing her own song. She refused the first eighteen times (as anyone might) when I requested this bespoke jig. But one night when she was about two, we had a musical breakthrough on a par with Susan Boyle chirping up on *Britain's Got Talent*. Mae unveiled a song about 'Stripey Stripes the Poo Zebra'. It was part rap, part nursery rhyme with a hint of the *PAW Patrol* theme tune.

It was pre-bath-time and she had abandoned her day-care-ravaged threads with wild abandon to start bouncing about, butt naked, rap rhymin' away until, inevitably, she collided with a rather angular toilet brush.

This led to inconsolable wailing and it seemed that Stripey Stripes the Poo Zebra was no more. But that's where the C word comes into its own: when you've had a run-in with some bog-cleaning equipment or you've fallen down trying to take those first steps and find yourself on the bathroom floor, thinking you were stupid for singing from another song sheet. That's when confidence steps up. It's not about wearing a swan-inspired frock like Björk, or delighting the crowds with your surprising package in the play *Equus* (thanks Daniel Radcliffe, quite the *Harry Potter* U-turn).

It's popping the toilet brush back into position, it's drying yourself (and the tears) off, remembering where you were pre-slippage, grabbing that song sheet – *your* song sheet – and continuing to sing horribly out of tune to the beat of your own drum.

It took two hours to get Mae confidently singing that Stripey ditty once more; in the past it has taken me weeks to bring myself back. But every peak has a trough, and without confidence you are left only with a soggy bit of lettuce in what could have been a triumphant BLT.

They will fall down numerous times trying to walk; *you* will struggle trying to talk through the exhaustion (I once found myself slurring like an alcoholic when asked what coffee I would like). But together you'll work it out, because Mae instilled as much confidence in me as I did in her.

Well, other than during one treacherous journey on the 55

bus to Leyton. Mae was a fully walking, talking human at this point and I contracted a gastro-bug while on 'watch' (parenting) and had to make it home from central London with a child, an abandoned scooter, a mouth brimming with saliva and a nappy bag bulging with life tat.

The journey usually takes thirty-one minutes; this onslaught took two hours fourteen minutes. It was how I'd imagine the urbanite's Duke of Edinburgh Award excursion. You've ransacked your 4G, you've got a raging three-year-old mainlining Cheetos, a vomming bug that requires access to a receptacle (or park bush) every fifteen minutes, and a veritable O_2 Arena's worth of people to quietly judge you along your merry way.

The 55 to Leyton was our chosen vehicle. Fearing containment on the Tube with a gastro-tsunami brewing, I thought the bus was the safest route – I couldn't face being the person who triggers the 'Could a member of the cleaning staff . . .' announcement.

By this point I'd lost the will to live – no different to anyone else on public transport in London at 6.01 p.m., really – and was now beset by the post-Cheeto toddler. Weak and clammy, I essentially handed over the parenting reins to the rest of that poor commuter-rammed bus and relinquished any hope that I'd come out of this with a Richard and Judy parenting rosette (if there was ever one; feels like there should be).

It started with some light planking. You know the sort: the kid arches away from the seat. I did nothing. Just sat there, staring ahead, trying not to explode, my focus mainly sphincter-related. Things then escalated quickly – Mae decided to empty a Tupperware of grapes onto the floor. I didn't flinch, I couldn't

– any sudden movement and the volcano could blow. I saw a fleet of those little fruits pinballing from foot to foot until one pinged off the immaculate L.K. Bennett heel of a body-conned-up-to-the-eyeballs city girl. Her disgust was palpable. Another grape gently nudged her Michael Kors tote as we took a bend with a little too much gusto.

There was a collective sigh of relief as Mae and I bundled off at the next stop so I could decorate a nearby alley that was usually reserved for 3 a.m. piss and Chicken Cottage debris.

We got on the next bus for a fresh troop of commuting comrades/victims. My thoughts edged once more to the uncontrollable rectal arena as my gag reflex started to spark up. 'Please can it not be the double,' I thought.

Then for the shame crescendo – and as parents we are not shame averse when you consider how the lil' scamps come into this world. I had to press the emergency button. The yellow one. The one that I'm constantly telling Mae not to touch because it's for world-altering police and fireman emergencies. I pressed it. Mae looked at me like I was a pioneer, the mothership going 'code yellow'.

The bus came to a shuddering halt just in time for me to get off and explode in the privacy of some Coke-can-embellished bush. I had no phone battery, no food for Mae (and I'd shat my undercrackers in some stabby part of East London). This was parenting on the front line. This was definitely not parenting the shit out of life.

By this point The People Of London had abandoned me entirely; I was one rung down from bag lady as I staggered around in an area that's neither up nor coming. And, of course, the rain came down and it was wetter than any rain I'd encountered.

'Mama, why do you smell of poo?'

But while tears were an obvious option at this juncture, I did what all parents eventually do – I offered up my last shred of dignity to get us over the final hurdle.

'Squidge, you are the mummy and I am the baby. You need to help get the baby home.'

Buoyed up by her new parental status, she took that abandoned scooter from my numb hand and gently edged me out of the park towards the bus stop.

We got onto that all-too-familiar 55 once more – I placed a Sainsbury's bag on the seat to save soiling – and we got home. We made it, we bagged that golden accolade, we staggered triumphantly through that domestic finish line.

And that's ultimately what counts with parenting: you get it done. It's never the meadowy, white-cotton-dress, skipping scene from *Little House on the Prairie*, and you sometimes feel like a sardine out of a tin (fish out of water sounds too perky). But you make it from A to B. As long as you come through that door at the end of the day with everyone vaguely alive, you've won – even if there has been public defecation. Even with the patronising back pat from my new 'mum': 'Well done baby, you did very well.'

Like all things when we get a bit smug, there's a moment where you come crashing back to earth to realise that you are just another dung beetle hauling that prized turd up a hill.

School uniform: the unwavering trends of motherhood

The minute you embark on parenting, your style doesn't suddenly dissolve. Well, it does a bit – I wore some jogging bottoms from 1996 for the best part of six months and found myself standing in a super-market in a leopard onesie two weeks in. But when you start to come through the maternal fug (it's always gonna be a little fuggy), there's a whole new world of STUFF. Stuff for mamas, stuff for kids, stuff for your home and stuff to Sellotape your face back together.

THE BRETON TOP

It's safe, it's versatile and it says might-be-a-bit-posh-or-am-I-hipster? Equally available in T.K. Maxx and Stella McCartney, it's a non-threatening nautical safe house for attracting all kinds of mum mates. The joy of the Breton top is it doesn't isolate any group, so if in doubt get yer Breton out.

MAC'S LADY DANGER LIPSTICK

If you're slathering on this pillar-box red lippy for the playground, you're not looking to welcome everyone into the nook. A slick of red lipstick pre-12 p.m. is the equivalent of cracking open the frizzante after brekkie on holiday. Essentially, it's a great idea but not everyone will approve. The irony of 'Lady Danger' among those of us who peel grapes and pop them into Tupperware is not lost. Dangerous, indeed.

THE DUNGAREE

While they might isolate close family members ('Darling, why are you dressed as a Minion?'), the dungaree has fast become the common style denominator across motherhood. Perfect for whapping a bap out to breastfeed, the dungaree says you're breezy, playful and probably a really good person. If the dungaree was an actual person it would be Holly Willoughby. Or, on a darker day when accessorised with Petits Filous, it might be Jason Donovan circa 1993 when he went full 'bad boy'.

THE MOTHER TEE

The Selfish Mother tee is the fashwan Sellotape holding us all together. It is motherhood style Mecca; an item that not only does good (profits go to Women for Women) but cuts through all the 'squad' stuff. The Mother Tee is everything we are; hardworking, goes-with-anything and will take you seamlessly from day to night (but not in a nightclub way; more a make-the-Sleep-Sheep-stop way).

Call 999: the common ways to 'break' a toddler

At two years old, Mae ended up in A&E with 'nurse-maid's elbow'. Nope, we hadn't heard of it before either. Here are a few common toddler emergencies that crop up in A&E on a daily basis:

ELBOW'S OUT

One, two, three . . . swing! It's an age-old game: two parents, one toddler and a swinging motion that usually leaves them gurning like a spangled Scot at Hogmanay. But this very movement makes all doctors weep into their stethoscopes – it's called 'nursemaid's elbow' and it's one of the most common kiddie A&E injuries. In short, any swift 'pulling' motion can dislodge the elbow from its socket and leave you with a wailing infant and a jaunt to A&E. And it takes up to five minutes for the kid to realise what has happened so you have NO IDEA what caused it unless you had previous knowledge of this stealth ailment.

FOLLICALLY CHALLENGED

Okay, so who knew a strand of hair could get so tightly wrapped around a baby's finger (or penis – jeez) and cut off circulation? It's called Hair-thread Tourniquet syndrome and happens a lot. It's like one of those unsolved mysteries – including necklaces that become entangled while stationary on your bedside table. Kid crying more than usual? Finger/toe/penis (jeez, once more) look a little purple? Get that urchin to hospital – your follicles are to blame.

SLIP SLIDIN'

You see it all the time: parents merrily swooping down a slide with urchin happily chirping on lap. Well, stop now parental folk. One of the biggest causes of broken legs in kids is this exact scenario. It starts with a rubber-soled shoe on your kid and ends in a painful heap at the bottom of this unassuming playground apparatus. If you insist on shoe-horning your derrière onto a children's slide, make sure the life project is fully boarded upon your lap, with no limbs/rubber soles in contact with the runway. You are welcome.

Papa Pukka.

The urchin had collapsed, slow and howling, to plant her face on the pavement. Her legs pounded up and down. With the ululating squawks and the rhythmic thumps, our eighteen-month-old sounded like a pterodactyl in a tumble dryer. The reason? I unscrewed the lid on her yoghurt pouch, the malevolent bastard that I am.

Fortunately, she had saved the show for the moment we walked past a rush-hour bus stop on a busy London high street. This way, my parenting 'skills' could be judged by a panel of strangers, through the medium of rolled eyes, blank scowls and, from one beige-coated old dear, an indulgent smile that said silently, 'This is what happens when men parent.'

Usually, this kind of meltdown can be handled using one of four of my trusted techniques:

1. Appeasement – the kind of preemptive surrender that would have made even Neville Chamberlain blush, this involves proffering juice, treats and my dignity in return for peace.
2. The scoop and stride – where I tuck her under my arm and carry on about my business while she flails around.
3. The lockdown – in this non-violent policing technique, I strap the resistant perp into her buggy, while she goes as limp as overdone spaghetti, like those Vietnam War protestors from the olden days.
4. The proper parent – a calm and patient explanation of the situation, and why her behaviour is unhelpful for either of us. This is, regrettably, rarely used.

But in a moment of desperate inspiration, I did something I promised I never would. I did something that I now realise is the go-to of loving but lost parents everywhere. I told a massive lie.

'Look: squirrel!' I said, pointing at a nearby tree.

The noise stopped. Her head rose: no squirrel here. As she drifted back to the pavement, I doubled down.

'Look! There she is. With a baby!'

Some bus-stop people also looked. The 'squirrel technique' was mesmeric.

'Squiwul?' Mae asked.

'She must have gone for her dinner,' I said. 'Shall we have some too?'

There was a pause, then a nod.

'Would you like to push the buggy?'

Another nod. A sniffle. I turned to the bus-stop people and smiled smugly. And then I wiped her nose with my hand, because I'd forgotten the wet wipes.

Such interactions had become a staple of my daily life. The move from baby-owner to toddler-wrangler made it clear to me just how little I knew, and how wrong I was in thinking that parenting might actually be a tiny bit easier than people made out.

Baby Mae could usually be placated with a cuddle or some milk or a nap. Toddler Mae had increasingly strident opinions about everything, from which feet her shoes should go on (usually the wrong ones) to acceptable colours for feeding spoons.

Watching a person develop is joyous, but getting them to eat, wear clothes and not smell bad is a slow psychological torture. Patience is key, but patience is not always possible when you have to get to work or catch a train, and hope also to eat, wear clothes and not smell bad yourself. Childcare manuals and well-meaning relatives talk about calm instruction and routine: these are admirable and sometimes achievable goals.

But sometimes, like when you're late for work, you have to accept that yours will be the child with unbrushed hair, or wearing a pendant of yoghurt stains. Some nights it'll be a quick dunk rather than a proper bath. Some nights it'll be neither. Some teeth might go unbrushed, because you can't forcibly clean someone's teeth without using mechanical clamps.*

Before becoming a parent, I had visions of myself as some kind of Wonder Dad: a quiet dispenser of justice and wisdom with smiley eyes and an even temperament. The kind of man who always had time for larking about on the swings, but could also offer moral guidance and toddler-friendly fairy tales about the importance of personal responsibility. The kind of man who no longer saw the need for hair wax, but still had effortlessly styled and very clean hair. I'd practised my kindly-wisdom voice and was even toying with the idea of chunky knitwear.

In practice, though, I tend to have ketchup on some of my clothing at all times and resort to poo gags and confectionery bribes at the slightest provocation. But I'm always aiming for (a little bit) more. I know it's important to be patient. I know it's important to speak kindly and be consistent; to reward good behaviour with encouraging words as enthusiastically as you chastise the outbreaks of mild hooliganism. But, sometimes, I need a bit more guidance than these generalisations, which is where the FBI comes in.

* Do not use mechanical clamps on children.

Hostage negotiations

On 9 September 1971, a thousand prisoners at the Attica Prison in New York rioted over conditions, taking forty-two hostages. After four days of 'negotiations' during which he refused to go to the prison and communicate with the prisoners directly, Governor Nelson Rockefeller sent in the troops. During the raid, thirty-three inmates and ten prison staff were killed. The botched rescue led the FBI to create the Behavioral Influence Stairway Model, which remains the basis for most hostage negotiations today (at least the ones where people don't want there to be shooting).

Hopefully, your home is not much like Attica Prison in the 1970s, your toddler is not a violent career criminal and you have more emotional intelligence than Governor Rockefeller.

Even so, there may be something from the FBI's techniques that transfers to stand-offs around tooth-brushing, sweet consumption or screen time. The difficulty of your role, as parent, is that you are both hostage and negotiator. The small person has taken your time and chunks of your sanity and only plans to relinquish them once their demands have been met.

You do have one thing to your advantage, however – these hostage-takers are not wild-eyed fundamentalists who think they are the instruments of some imagined almighty. Hopefully.

These are more like bank robbers in a predicament – all they really want is for their life to be nicer, and they believe unmarked bills (Haribo/another cartoon/not wearing a coat) will achieve this. People who want something can be negotiated with, which is why some 85 per cent of hostage situations are resolved successfully.

According to Randall Rogan, a professor in crisis communications at Carolina's Wake Forest University, 'time, in almost all these situations, is the ally of law enforcement. As time passes and the hostage remains unharmed, the hostage-taker is likely calming down.'

But time is one thing that parents just don't have enough of, so here is my accelerated version of the Behavioural Influence Stairway Model for parents.

ACTIVE LISTENING

Also known as 'giving it the big eyes', this is the first stage in gaining the perp's trust. Ask what's up. Nod a little and paraphrase what they've said, in a sympathetic manner. For real hostage negotiators, this is the most important part and can take hours, but remember, toddlers work in a hyperspeed alternative reality, so you might get away with 'You don't want to wear shoes today?' (make a sad face).

EMPATHY

While every fibre of your core may want to just Sellotape the chuffing shoes to your tiny despot and leave the house, the Feds would advise 'emotional labelling' at this point, and giving the perp's feelings validity: 'Sometimes it does feel unfair that we have to wear shoes.' Continue with the big eyes. I find it helps at this point to imagine I'm a kindly old aunt character in a Mexican telenovela, fixed in a close-up as I do 'concerned face'.

MIRRORING

I have embellished the FBI approach with an extra stage that Anna uses with some success. When faced with outright mutiny, while I am doing silent swears in my head, Anna often leads with something like, 'When I was little, I didn't always want to wear a coat', as an extra empathetic layer to get our tiny perp on side.

RAPPORT

This is the part in the films where the sweaty-pitted bank robber and the crumpled-shirted hostage negotiator exchange tales of their ex-wives. Once you've established a common feeling (ambivalence to coats) you can establish a common goal (not catching a cold). If you've gone with, 'I also didn't like wearing coats', you might follow up with a tale of how you caught a cold and missed a party/caught scurvy/stood shivering in the street like a Dickensian waif.

INFLUENCE

With trust established, you can move the conversation on to achieving your shared goal, such as getting to day-care to play with so-and-so (weird name for a child). You will then all skip gaily outside, your nipper suitably wrapped up against the elements.*

Now, there are certain flaws here. FBI negotiators want to prolong discussions for hours or days, and as a parent, you

---

* Gaily skipping outside not guaranteed.

will generally have a few minutes. But the behaviour stairway can be condensed. If, for example, the issue is an urgent demand for a magazine while queuing at the till in the super-market, you might run through the following:

'You want a magazine?' (Active listening)

'I'd quite like one too.' (Empathy)

'But Mummy's got dinner at home, and she'll be upset if we're too busy reading to eat.' (Rapport)

'And if we don't get this carrot/cooking oil/lavender-scented-centrepiece-candle back quickly, dinner will be ruined.' (Influence and solution to shared goal)

In theory, this will then lead to behaviour change and less grizzling about the *Kartoonz* mag that's just out of their sticky little reach.

Of course, bank robbers are more rational than toddlers and most psychiatrists reckon that kids don't develop full reasoning skills until they're about seven. If it all goes wrong, the parental equivalent of sending in the SWAT team is to pop your coatless spawn over your shoulder and head out the door, coat to be applied at a later stage (probably when they realise how chuffing cold it is).

Second-choice parent

When Mae was about two, we went away for Easter with some friends. They had a boy about the same age as her and we rented a cottage down a little wooded path in the middle of nowhere. It backed on to a forest perfect for Easter egg hunts, and we arrived with a boot-full of food, chocolate, beer and wine.

Mae was going through a phase of saying, loudly and frequently, 'I don't like you; I want Mama.' For much of that weekend, if I tried to pick her up she would wriggle and squeal and want to get away. She would slap me in the face and reach out for Anna, or any other grown-up in the room, including the hairy chops of my mate Joe. She did, one evening, allow me to read the bedtime story, like a benevolent monarch who has decided to accept a garland from the proles. That weekend established for me very clearly that I was the second-favourite parent. In many cases, I was the least-preferred adult of any sort in the room and that lasted for a few months. It meant that only Anna could soothe Mae when she was having tantrums and we would often just give in when faced with 'Mama do it' rages over who tackled bath time or getting Mae dressed. It left me feeling quietly resentful that Mae was throwing my best parenting efforts back at me, and caused friction between me and Anna as she was forced to take on more of the rearing, often with me standing there trying to contribute but being about as useful to the parenting process as a vintage lampshade.

But this is, the quacks say, a fairly common phase. Toddlers want to assert their independence and choosing one parent over the other is part of that as much as developing a favoured sippy cup. (I am the slightly melted plastic Tommee Tippee item at the back of the cupboard, while Anna is the Spiderman slurpee beaker with built in swirly straw.)

But it's also a stage when they're developing empathy for others. Around that time, there was a moment when Mae's three-year-old cousin started blubbing over his dinner, so she hopped off Anna's lap, saying, with the quiet confidence of a master architect assessing a wonky roof, 'I better give him a cuddle.'

Partly, Anna was the chosen one because, well, she's the mum. She did the hard yards with the pregnancy and the breast-feeding. She also smells nice. Partly, I think it was because I was a little distracted. I was working most weekends, tackling emails in the evenings, and generally a bit emotionally absent.

I tried to make up for that by acting like a loyal collie that just wants to be by its master's side (the master, in this case, being a two-year-old prone to outrageous tantrums). If she made commands I would scamper off, metaphorical tail wagging, to fetch juice or trim the crusts of her toast. I made sure she asked properly, in sentences that ended with 'please', but there's no doubt about it: I was fetcher, gopher and bum-wiper, but not her number-one choice for any of these tasks.

And this is, I think, something most dads have to accept. Your kids will love you (hopefully), but in any fictional one-spare-seat-on-the-lifeboat scenario, they'd probably suggest that you chance your arm (literally) with the sharks and let

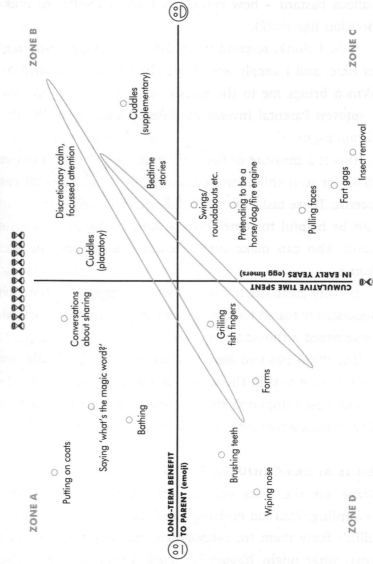

The Parental Investment Returns Matrix

ZONE A

ZONE B

ZONE C

ZONE D

Putting on coats

Conversations about sharing

Saying 'what's the magic word?'

Bathing

Brushing teeth

Wiping nose

Forms

Grilling fish fingers

Cuddles (placatory)

Discretionary calm, focussed attention

Cuddles (supplementary)

Bedtime stories

Swings/ roundabouts etc.

Pretending to be a horse/dog/fire engine

Pulling faces

Fart gags

Insect removal

CUMULATIVE TIME SPENT IN EARLY YEARS (egg timers)

LONG-TERM BENEFIT TO PARENT (emoji)

Mummy hop in (which you probably should anyway, you callous bastard – how could you force a toddler to make a decision like *that?*).

Kids, I think, respond more than anything to investments of time, and I simply wasn't spending much time with Mae. Which brings me to the utterly unscientific and completely unproven Parental Investment Returns Matrix (or PIRM; see facing page).

This is a measure of the time spent doing various parental tasks for your child, and the long-term benefits to you as the parent. These tasks often feel laborious and thankless, but it can be helpful to remember the end goal – a well-rounded adult who can make sure you don't get abused in a care home.

If every great journey begins with a single step, then every successfully reared toddler begins with a changed nappy, via a nose wiped a thousand times.

The PIRM has two axes: the horizontal indicates the long-term benefit to you. The vertical is a measure of the time spent doing these things over the first few years of your nipper's life. These break down into the following four zones:

ZONE A: BASIC HOUSEKEEPING

These are the tasks that are time-consuming but not so rewarding. Your kid probably needs to wear a coat. But if you didn't force them to, every single morning for most of the year, what might happen? A cold, perhaps? Maybe they'd more quickly develop an ability to judge whether or not they need a coat? At least 46 per cent* of the reason why parents make their children wear coats is so other parents don't judge them.

ZONE B: THE IMPORTANT BITS

This is the big stuff, the bits they remember. These are the deposits into the bank of emotional wellbeing of a future adult. Unless you have a particularly heinous technique, no grown-up will remember all the times you wiped their nose as a child. But they will remember the bedtime stories and silly voices, or the time spent quietly colouring in with them, or listening while they tell you about their favourite member of Paw Patrol/Power Rangers/The Famous Five. Even if they don't recall the specifics, it'll be in there somewhere and make them less likely to cash in your savings when the dementia takes hold. Those thin oblongs are so stretched because focused attention has a direct return on your time investment. The more you put in, the more you get back in the end, like compound interest.† Also note the varied cuddle types. The placatory cuddles (i.e. little Jonny has grazed his knee or lost his bunny) are most frequent, but I think the supplementary ones (the ones that happen just because) have more impact.

* This is made up.

† The value of investment in children can go down as well as up. Your emotional capital is at risk. Some kids will become horrible humans regardless of a loving upbringing. (But I reckon that's pretty rare.)

ZONE C: THE WIN ZONE

These are easy wins. Making a fart noise takes approximately two seconds and has never failed to win the affection of a single human toddler.* Insect removal, especially if done with minimum fuss and calm competence (rather than screaming like a goose yourself), will mark you out as a quiet hero. It's really the dadding equivalent of being a firefighter. Honestly, I catch a spider in a glass about once every six months for Mae and every time I walk away feeling like a fricking dragon slayer.

ZONE D: DRUDGE CORNER

The dull bits: form-filling, nose-wiping and the daily battle of the toothbrush. Dental hygiene costs me about twenty minutes a day, and will almost certainly have no impact on our relationship in later life. But dentists say we must, so we must. (I mean, I assume we must. These are milk teeth after all. You don't decorate when you're renting, do you?)

Basically, all the things are important but our time is short, and I suspect nothing is more important than focused attention.

What happens when?

I spent the first two years of Mae's life wondering when she might be able to catch a ball (about three, it turns out). It's been said by many parents before me,

* Research incomplete at time of press.

but each new stage, every new skill, however trivial-seeming, is a glorious thing to see and likely to cause a silent surge of soppy pride.

Here's a short list of when toddlers will typically do things by, adapted from NHS and Baby Centre info. But don't worry too much if yours is out of step. Babies and toddlers develop at different rates, and some nippers skip crawling completely to suddenly spring to their feet at one year old. If you're concerned, speak to your doctor. Otherwise, here's a rough guide.

THIRTEEN MONTHS
Can use one or two words (hopefully not swears). Stands up, before collapsing like a drunken sailor.

FOURTEEN MONTHS
Shovels food into own face, a bit like a drunken sailor. Pours drinks on the floor, laughs heartily about results. Copies others' actions and words (hopefully not swears).

FIFTEEN MONTHS
Might say five or more words (fingers crossed, still no swearing). Staggers backward (pretty amazing to see, although still quite 'drunken sailor-ish').

SIXTEEN MONTHS

Flips pages of baby books, regardless of what bit you're reading.

Launches into comedy strops when things aren't working out.

SEVENTEEN MONTHS

Starts to combine words (e.g., 'go 'way', 'don't want').

Rides around on toys (i.e. you).

EIGHTEEN MONTHS

Pedals on a trike (often into you).

Scribbles on important presentations, rare prints, treasured LPs.

Has strong opinions about suitable attire.

NINETEEN MONTHS

Can use a spoon and fork (boom! You've got a self-feeder, congratulations).

Can run (buy plasters).

Can throw a ball underarm (now you're parenting).

TWENTY MONTHS

Pretends to feed dolls (awww, *kewt!*).

Puts things in the bin. (Congratulations, you now have a domestic aid. Do not be shy about assigning 'fun' tasks. Around this stage, one sunny Sunday in their garden, Anna's mum gave Mae a bucket of water and a brush, and asked her to 'paint' the outside of the house. It was a blissful thirty minutes of peace for us and concentrated achievement for her, because, of course, as the water dries the work needs repeating, like a toddler-friendly version of painting the Forth Road Bridge.)

TWENTY-ONE MONTHS
Stairs!

TWENTY-TWO MONTHS
Balls! Kicking!

TWENTY-THREE MONTHS
Has a vocabulary of fifty or more words (has surpassed a drunken sailor).
Can build towers with a few bricks (has surpassed a drunken sailor).

TWENTY-FOUR MONTHS
Forms sentences ('I want more juice!' – hopefully still swear-free and occasionally using 'please').

10

A happy ending

Mother Pukka.

I think I forgot about the mind/fanny/abdomen-altering trauma of childbirth around the time I located my FDPs (Friday Disco Pants). They're a kaleidoscopic triumph and made of some sort of shiny Spandex that mysteriously flatters even the most bulging derrière. Think palm trees, galaxies and rainbows and you've got some idea of the power of these trews. If My Little Pony created a pair of pants that epitomised the brand's multi-hued DNA, these would be them.

I first wore them to a house party in 2002, when I ended up in hospital after having my head accidentally shut in a door by my housemate. I remember nothing other than those glorious pants.

The FDPs have always drawn a crowd. I wore them pre-pregnancy on special occasions – birthday, best friend's birthday, the postman's birthday, that time when Kerry Katona won *I'm a Celebrity* – and I wore them during pregnancy because they reminded me of Friday-disco-times as I was waddling about the supermarket on the hunt for spuds to mash for tea.

But since having Mae, they had been buried underneath layers of safer fashion items – the boyfriend jean, the afore-mentioned dungarees and Breton top, and a heap of greying Primark tees. These maternal stalwarts had gradually edged the FDPs out of the wardrobe due to dwindling confidence on my side.

Until Mae dragged them out one day (having released almost every other garment in the process) and held them up for me to wear. With Disney-esque eyes, she hollered, 'Mama, Mama, Mama' and then, when I didn't swoop upon them like a well-trained Crufts contender, 'Mama-aaaaaa-aaaaa!'

So to keep her schtum, I slipped into those jazzy leggings – made for dark disco nights rather than bright playground days – and fuelled by half a warm Babybel, we went to the park.

I don't know if I scuppered any potential friendships – there was a curmudgeonly-looking nanny with her troupe and a pale-faced dad there, so I assume not – but it sure felt good to relight that psychedelic fire. I think, looking back, it was then that I felt ready to 'try' for number two. To bonk with intent once more and have those jazzy leggings awkwardly dragged off my lumpy post-partum booty as we had a go at making another small human.

How hard can two be, I thought. I've managed to keep one alive for 756 days – perhaps that was a test run and I'd be really good at this one. I think Matt felt the same. He didn't articulate as much but he'd been gyrating behind me as I unloaded the dishwasher more than usual.

(Am I alone in this sporadic, kitchen-based gyrating? The more people I speak to about this primitive act, the more admit to being domestically dry humped. Is scrubbing a stubborn grain of porridge from your IKEA bowls really the red light for 'Let's get it on?' Are marigolds the new knee-highs? Does Fairy Liquid have the same allure as Durex's 'hot 'n' spicy' lube?)

But why do we even do it? I mean the human end-result of the *it*. The whole 'tick tock' urge is a complete myth according to science, and the internet answered my base question of 'why do people *want* to have children' with the following:

- Creating children contributes to the human race's survival. (I agree with this one, yet not everyone is obliged to do so with the current population of seven billion living persons.)

- Children's loveliness makes parents happy. (At times, yes. Less so when having Weetabix smashed into your face by a feral toddler.)

- Children can take care of their parents when they grow old. (A well-developed modern society should be able to do this without much difficulty.)

- Children add freshness to the family. (Is 'fresh' really the right word in the face of a bin overflowing with sodden nappies?)

• Raising a child successfully fulfils one's unrealised goals/ unsatisfied dreams/ego. (It's probably time to give up on those dreams of being a Premier League football player when you get a bead-on running for the bus.)

No, for us, the truth of the matter was we wanted to see what another one would look like. And then see what it sounds like. And then how it lives. And how it lives with Mae. It was simple – we wanted to watch our kids grow up. For all the eye-twitching, mind-numbing madness associated with parenting, it's like watching your favourite Netflix series unfurl over a lifetime.

There are bonkers characters, plot twists and turns, the scenery shifts every season and you often teeter between laughter and tears as you become so hooked on an episode that you forget to put knickers on that day. (Not in the 'come hither' way; more in the forgetfulness way.)

It's also the ultimate vanity project, where you give your all for little more than sporadic hugs. Essentially, we wanted more of us in the world. But mostly we wanted more of each other out there, because for all the griping and low-level angst about who has put the spatula in the wrong drawer, making a baby stems from a place of genuine affection. Matt is my mate.

Having another one felt like remembering the best bits of *The Sopranos* (they were such a lovely family, really), while ignoring the times when someone's head got smashed against a pavement.

Having 'produced' a kid that looked identical to Matt (from the heavy Celtic eyebrows – quite Cara Delevingne – to the oversized gap between her first and second toe), I also wanted another throw of the DNA dice. I think it was when a friend said 'she definitely has your shoulders' that I decided I wanted more of a biological look-in this time.

So, knowing the potentially dodgy path that lay ahead after having lost a few little lives along the way to Mae, we boldly cast aside the Durex and went at it like, well, overtired hamsters. Working full time with a toddler in tow, you are unlikely to be able to keep up with the more rampant rabbit.

The biggest surprise was how hard it was actually to get our bits together this time round. It required the scheduling of a frazzled Biology teacher in a school that has been wildly over-subscribed. The first time we 'tried' before Mae stuck, we had all the time in the world to hump away freely until the reproductive cogs worked. There was even time for down and dirty weekend breaks focused solely on bumping uglies in the hope that I'd leave up the duff.

This time round it was a case of slip it in before one of us falls asleep. I even remember saying to Matt he could keep going if I'd nodded off (he promises he didn't). Truly romantic, mildly narcoleptic times.

There was also the pocket of flesh that hung over my C-section scar to contend with. The word 'flap' is not something that makes you feel particularly ready to pull out the sexy-time moves.

While body confidence is not something I question – Head? Good. Legs? Work. Bottom? Definitely there – mine isn't the vaguely toned body of the first time we went for it. It was all a little more on the move second time round – a bit like the effects of jumping on a waterbed. There was a definite ripple effect.

Second time round I abandoned any chaffing frilly knickers and fake tan in exchange for having a shower and not smelling like an old sock. My legs being shaved was the green light, while a spiky pair of pins and pyjamas buttoned up to the eyeballs generally meant 'do not enter'. Our bed was also a lot creakier than in Amsterdam, so we tended to accommodate the creaks with a lower tempo, which meant we were trying to have sex slowly, hoping not to break the bed or wake the child. I reiterate: romantic times.

There is nothing stranger than having sex when there's a kid in the next room. There had been something mildly exciting about having quiet sex with Matt when we were staying with his folks. But quiet sex when there's a toddler in the next room is just traumatic. It's laced with so much fear of scarring them for life or, worse, having to answer awkward questions should they walk in at the moment of no return. Mae had already asked at this point why 'Papa has a willy' and I was keen to leave that line of interrogation there. (A friend of ours had a three-year-old daughter who was doing the 'hoo-ha shuffle', where she'd edge herself around the carpet without her pants on and say 'my hoo-ha feels funny'. When they asked her to stop, she asked 'Why?' and I still don't think they've found an answer.)

It was on a weekend visiting my sister and her girlfriend in

Amsterdam that I knew I was pregnant again. I was looking like I had the after-party bloat – puffy face, lacklustre eyes and disinterest in the human race without a caffeine boost every hour or so. I did the test, the line was clear, it was affirmative: we were knocked up and like an old nag staring out onto the Grand National course, I was vaguely ready to go again. I saddled up for the ride and decided once again to take each furlong at a time.

But that initial excitement was halted in its tracks before we were even out of the starting blocks. I lost that pregnancy two weeks later. It was rubbish, I sat in that familial dark hole again ('It's common' never seemed to help when seeing doctors) and then I got back on the horse once more and we got pregnant two months later – a pregnancy we also frustratingly, upsettingly and heartbreakingly lost.

It was on holiday in Menorca as I was eating a fairly limp salad niçoise when I felt the familiar blood between my thighs. I was seven weeks pregnant and I knew, despite wild denial, that it was happening again.

We had rented a little villa, so my mum and dad were with me along with Mae and Matt. On that overcast Menorcan day, pierced with occasional squeals from giddy children in a nearby swimming pool, I calmly uttered the words to my ma that every pregnant woman fears: 'I'm bleeding.'

I think it was in that moment that I realised that I wasn't alone in emotionally ricocheting between faux positivity – Googling all possible positive outcomes when bleeding – and crippling fear.

The truth is that however supportive my dad, husband, friends and sister were, you don't understand the searing pain of losing a child unless you've been there. A name has been imagined, that foetus is a person, a member of the family – 'the newest recruit' as Matt would say.

'We will take every day as it comes,' Mum responded in a voice I hadn't heard since I was a child and being read *The Curly Cobbler* (a favourite book about an old mouse that made spectacular shoes). It was a mix of fierce protectiveness and quiet calm. I felt the maternal wing swoop over me and I instantly became childlike myself; the foetal position helped both cramps and emotions.

Few words were spoken during the days that followed; our communication would manifest itself more physically – a gentle arm squeeze, a furtive glance when I'd returned from the toilet. My mum knew from her own experience of loss that no words can placate the numbing fear and potential lost dreams. There was no bedtime story that could take away the emptiness that was about to descend as the final thread of hope was flushed down the toilet. My mum knew to sit in the dark hole with me.

On our return from that holiday she decided to stay one more night at our London home. I think she knew from her own experience that I hadn't yet hit rock bottom – that I was still unable to accept the reality of two more embryos missing the mark. She also knew I was measuring up those losses with the love I felt for Mae – what I was losing felt more painful looking into her eyes every day.

In an attempt to push my feelings away, I decided to re-tile the kitchen floor at 4 p.m. Matt protested and that's when my mum intervened – 'We'll do it together; it will be okay' – before setting off to B&Q with the frenzied determination of a starved mosquito.

We sweated away until the early hours, mildly sunburnt from Menorca and both determined to finish the daunting DIY task in front of us. Somewhere between unearthing a damp, mouldy 1976 *Waltham Forest Echo* that had been used as floor insulation and asking Mum to pass me a chisel, I broke down. It was a deep-seated grief for all the five children I had lost. She held me in a vice-like grip until I couldn't cry any more and I knew something had shifted. I was no longer alone as we mourned both our losses as mother and daughter; one woman holding another. 'You happened when I had almost given up,' she told me on one of the days that followed.

But it was Mae who finally pulled me out of the dark fug of loss a few days later. It was this line of interrogation on the Central line with a rammed carriage of people that finally turned the tears to laughter:

'Mama, why were you just crying?'
[Whispered] 'Well, the baby that was in Mummy's tummy is no longer there.'
'Did the baby fall out?'
'Erm, yes; sometimes through no fault of your own, a baby doesn't stay in.'
'Can the doctor put a new one in?'

'I'll need to discuss that with Papa, really.'
'Can the next one be black?'
'Again, I'll need to discuss that with Papa, poppet.'

After that intense Tube journey, it was ten months later that I gave birth to our daughter Eve. Laughter combined with giving up hope seemed to be the miracle fix.

We were to be parents once more.

I would say at this juncture that despite all the great things my mum did to look after my sister and me over the years, perhaps the one thing that sticks out was that she always served up the shitty, crusty, burnt bit of lasagne for herself, leaving the rest of us with the best slabs (though she always gave herself the nicest wine glass).

That's what I came to learn about parenthood from my own parents in those first few years: it is about putting your family first but not at the cost of your own mind.

It's when you've had two hours thirty-four minutes of sleep and your newborn has been mewling like a sad vole, and somewhere in there you have a piece of toast and feel like a champion.

It's when you face a salivary-gland-igniting nappy situation in a train toilet and realise there's virtually no situation a baby wipe can't fix.

It's when you've been in a postnatally depressed fug and find mild humour in a takeaway ad that says: 'I've . . . had . . . the Thai of my life.'

It's when you've given, given and given once more and are on the brink of maternal collapse in the frozen goods aisle of Tesco and you get a spontaneous shin cuddle from your previously planking toddler.

It's when you find yourself chewing on that slab of burnt lasagne but have a slug of above-average rioja and feel like an absolute winner.

It's when you find yourself as a mother, wiping away the tears of your thirty-five-year-old daughter and realising that parenting is not a sprint, but more of a long-distance run with no finish line.

It's for all those moments you've wildly questioned mind, fanny and soul and realised that you are, in fact, parenting the shit out of life.

Papa Pukka.

Until Mae turned two, I thought one child might be enough. We'd got through the sleepless nights and her personality was developing. We had reached a manageable rhythm where one of us would parent while the other worked or ran errands or, even occasionally, entertained themselves with grown-up pleasures like reading the paper or going out with friends or idly scratching their plums on the sofa.*

We'd had three miscarriages before Mae came along and a

* Anna does not have plums.

couple of scares during our pregnancy with her, and the prospect of trying for, and losing, another baby was something that lingered in the backs of our minds and the pits of our stomachs. And so, for the first year at least, we settled on the idea of her being an only child.

But then two things happened. The first was that, along with the personality, our two-year-old was developing strident opinions on such significant matters as spoon colours and trousers choices, and would have the kind of red-cheeked tantrums rarely seen on anyone other than a Major League Baseball coach.

The other was that, in spite of this, we began to wonder what another one might be like – what it would be like to have a tiny, frail, snuffling personlet again. In the time it had taken for Mae to reach advanced toddlerdom, we had forgotten what the first year or so had been like. Looking back at pictures of her as a newborn wrapped in wool, or first managing to lift her head, or crawling across the floor like she was surmounting her own personal Everest, was a curiously detached process. It was like we were looking back at past lives because, despite being just a few months ago, those moments felt like a distant memory. Despite all our better judgement, we were curious about experiencing those moments again.

We thought, naively perhaps, that having a sibling battling for our attention and resources might make Mae less demanding. It might teach her more about sharing and caring for others. Even if it did none of those things, it would give her an on-demand playmate for those times when sticklebricks were not enough.

We saw friends have their second children, or even their third. We saw that, among the tantrums and the tears, the siblings would play and laugh.

And so we went again. There were two more early-stage miscarriages, each one a thud that brought back all the others. And then there was one that stuck. We made the twelve-week scan and there was a little spike of hope. So we paid for more scans every couple of weeks, becoming addicted to the reassurance of that dark room and seeing the development of the little oblong being on the screen. And with each one of those visits, against my better judgement, I began to imagine what might be. We had learnt to set our hearts to 'let's wait and see', but each new scan made it more real. And then at twenty weeks, we were back in the hospital with the chance to discover the gender.

I had wanted a boy, of course, because all men do. I'm not sure why, but there's some lingering vanity about the family name and about creating someone in your own image. It feels the closest we might get to being god-like. But it also meant that I would have a recipient for my hard-won years of male-specific advice, like how to shave and how to avoid inner-trouser trickle-down.

The doc asked if we wanted to know, and when we said yes, he smiled absently at the screen and said, 'It's a girl.'

I grinned at Anna, who asked if I was okay, and I laughed and said, 'Of course', but there was a quiet lull in my heart.

A little flicker of, 'Oh well, no son for me.' It was swiftly gone but undeniably there.

Very occasionally, when I'm being dive-bombed by my nephew or I see a friend's boys and their relentless, gormless need to run and crash and clatter, that flicker returns. It's a feeling that comes and goes in a microsecond, in and out before the brain can address it.

But it's not a thing that lingers. It ebbed rapidly away with every thud of that tiny heart the moment the doctor turned on the audio of the ultrasound. What I wanted was a healthy baby, ready to nuzzle in to the space we had all created in our family.

We had many more scans, at our insistence and that of the doctors. We had two pre-term stays in hospital when it seemed the baby might be coming a little too soon. Every day brought the quiet worry that something might be wrong, and because the three pregnancies came in quick succession, we were pregnant for most of a fifteen- or sixteen-month period.

We ripped out our damp-infused kitchen and knocked down the outdoor toilet, the 'twelve-week' job beginning at twenty-eight weeks pregnant because we couldn't get the money together any sooner and we didn't want to believe a baby was coming until we could be sure. We grew ratty with each other because we were both afraid, and closer to each other when we admitted that.

And then, in June 2017, almost four years after her sister was born, Eve joined the clan: a little under 3 kg of snuffling perfection.

Between 2009 and 2016, the average age gap between siblings in Britain rose by five months, to three years and eight months.

It's not completely clear why. Partly, perhaps, it's because women are having children later and that can make conceiving more difficult. Partly, perhaps, it's to lessen the impact on the careers of parents. Maybe it's economic worries in the long, slow echo of the 2008 crash. There are some that believe it's best to 'get them all out of the way', so they'll be of an age where they have similar interests and you can shift them out of the nest in relatively short order at the other end. There are those who reckon that a bigger gap means more support-iveness between young and old siblings and an easier workload for the parents. Like most things to do with parenting, it's a bit of guesswork.

But since the moment I knew that Mae would have a sister, and knew as well what that rough age gap would be, I have hoped that the relationship that develops is something like the one between Anna and her (five years younger) sister, Karen.

My first experience of Karen came a couple of weeks after Anna and I started going out. She was curious about the guy that wanted to whisk her sister away to live abroad after only a few weeks together, and eager to put him to the test. We were meeting in a West London pub. It was a place where the girls all wore pashminas and the guys all looked like they'd stepped out of dress-down-Friday at an investment bank (mostly because they had).

Karen was wearing a shark hat. It had a foam tail that dangled down between her shoulder blades, and a wonky fin that added about 30 cm to her height. When I mentioned this, she asked if I'd like to wear it. Sensing this might be some kind of test, I did, while she quizzed me about my intentions towards Anna. It became clear over the following weeks that their relationship was consistently ridiculous.

Within seconds of seeing each other they would fall into conspiratorial giggles. They would exchange self-deprecating tales of what they'd been up to, interrupted only by extravagant praise delivered from one to the other.

They would paw enthusiastically at each other's clothes and deliver deliberately over-the-top compliments, broken up with mild ribbing about how nerdy they were as children, how awkward as adolescents, or reminisce about the hamster grave-yard at the bottom of the family garden.

It didn't matter if they were talking about the inanity of a recent bus journey or a life-changing event – their eyes were alight as they spoke to each other and there were times when all you could do was look on as a silent spectator. They called each other Skrinky and Ace, names that have no explanation to this day, and I became aware for the first time what sisterly relationships could be.

There was enough of an age gap to mean they were never competing over boys or exam results or sporting achievements, but it was close enough for them to be each other's closest confidantes and truest support. That, I thought, is what I want for my daughters.

Daughters, then

A few weeks after moving into our ramshackle terrace, we started Mae at a new nursery. The first days took some adjustment, and she would cry as we dropped her off. In the corner of the room they had a large box of dinosaurs and a large box of dolls.

At home, Mae had dinosaur toys, a dinosaur outfit, and did an impressive dinosaur 'Rarrr!' complete with clawing action.

So as she wailed and clung on as I went to leave, I tried to stop her tears by goofily waving a stegosaurus about. But her key worker, a quick-to-smile twenty-something (who, disconcertingly, called me 'Dad'), immediately resorted to the pink stuff.

'Shall we change the dolly's nappy?' she asked. 'Do you want to push the pram?'

And I wanted to say, 'Don't do that.' But being English, I gave an awkward smile and left her to it. A Monday morning, with work waiting, didn't seem the best time to launch into a half-considered speech on gender roles.

I'd been quiet on this before. When relatives hand over ulcer-pink dolly sets or the kind of frilly princess outfits that would shame a young Barbara Cartland, I smile, say thanks, and quietly shunt them to the back of the cupboard.

It's not an effort to deny Mae a girlhood, but more an attempt to offer her options. If she likes dolls, she can have dolls, but I'll point out a toy truck as well. I want her to be as quick to pick up a ball as a Barbie, as confident at a lectern as in a kitchen. I want her to hit back if struck.

And it occurred to me that I might have accidentally become a feminist, so I looked the word up for the first time. I was half expecting to see a picture of a hairy-pitted harridan, or a definition that ran along the lines, 'make-up-averse man-hater, wild-eyed castrator, gender bigot'.

Without thinking about it too much, I'd accepted the meaning that's hinted at by most media portrayals: someone who believes in the primacy of women over men, a pro-female discriminator.

But it said, simply, 'a person who supports women's rights on the ground of the equality of the sexes'.

And so, I thought, I guess I'm one of those then. Should I tell my mates? What will people think? Do I need to 'come out' or should I just keep it to myself? It's a socially awkward thing to say, and the 'ist' words are rarely positive: facist, racist, fantasist. Cyst.

But then I thought, well, how could you not be? If feminists believe in gender equality, then not being one means you actively believe in inequality: that blue is better than pink, so let's keep the boys in charge.

From the moment Mae arrived, and even more since Eve joined us, I've become aware of what women face and the way we speak to girls. The judgement that screams at them from so many news outlets, the expectations farted out by so many lame ads. The unthinking, habitual phrases we use and the subtly different expectations we set.

One recent study, conducted by some boffins at the University of Arizona, studied fifty-two dads (thirty with girls and twenty-two with boys) by strapping little mics to them for a week. The kids were all under two.

The dads with girls sang more and used more language related to the body and to sadness. They were more attentive, and used more analytical language. The dads of sons did more rough and tumble and used more language about achievement.

I wonder if I do things like this and if they are positive or harmful. I wonder how best I can help nurture confident and capable young women who want to work hard, have empathy for others and can tell filthy jokes. Who can be happy with who they are and happy too for others. I wonder how to get the message across, and what the message should be. I wonder how they'll be as teenagers and what relationshships we'll have left at the other end.

And all of these thoughts and questions sit in my head every day, sporadically popping to the surface when I'm going to work or making food or gazing like a lobotomised owl at my offspring.

National treasure David Attenborough once said that his favourite animal is a nine-month-old baby human. They were, he said, 'the only creature that really makes my jaw sag so much that I find it hard to stop looking'.

But my feeling is that this doesn't stop at nine months. It is the way I have looked at Mae and Eve since they first joined us. Anna has called me up on it before – a kind of weird gawp that looks like a cross between awe and constipation. It is not helped by the fact that my part-Scottish heritage gives me the complexion of a girder and the grimace of a computer programmer. Most of the time, I'm just trying to work out what the flying chuff

I'm supposed to be doing. What follows is my best guess and I reckon most of it applies to boys just as much as girls.

What I think I should tell my daughters

Perhaps they'd be better off – stronger, smarter and more self-assured – if I let them work things out for themselves. But that takes time, and they'll have other things to focus on, so here's what I think I should tell them.

To question everything, much as it might make my life difficult, because there's a lot to be said for understanding that you don't need to do things just because people tell you to,* and when quizzed you'd be surprised how many people turn out to to be making things up as they go along.

That their bodies are their own, and if they don't want to give Uncle Bert a goodbye kiss they don't have to.

That affection is not currency.

That girls can have a firm handshake too: not the white-knuckle grip of an insecure alpha politician, but one that says, 'I'm here', rather than, 'I'd prefer to curtsey.'

To know the way home, wherever you go.

That the first time someone hits you, you tell them never to do it again. The second time, you tell the teacher. And if it happens again, you have to hit back, and when you do, it's best to commit.

That people will call them cute, and say 'Aren't you pretty?'

* Exceptions include tooth-brushing, coat-wearing.

whenever they wear a party dress. And while that's fine, it is not the only praise to crave.

That young men are mostly idiots, but much of that comes from the expectation that they will be: expectations from their mates and movies and the images they see and whatever flaccid-hearted corner of the internet is telling them to 'man up'. But when the idiotic parts are pointed out to them, the good ones tend to reconsider.

To always have your share of the bill covered.

That you're better off alone than with the wrong person, because who you are is fine and time spent with the wrong person is time spent hiding from the right one.

To regularly scare yourself, by trying things you don't understand.

To work hard and be nice to people, and to save some money, just in case.

What I think I should show my daughters

These are the harder parts, because they rely on me doing things rather than dishing out vague parenting truths. If nothing else, having kids has forced me to be a better person by being more patient. I'm a man who is inclined to swear easily at malfunctioning technology and tools, but I'm having to learn to take a breath and favour reason over rages – to accept that calmness trumps tantrums and whatever the situation, you can keep a calm head. I'm hoping they'll pick up on that, but you never know.

But I'm also hoping to show them how they should expect to be treated. I'm aware that in some small way, dads provide part of the template for their daughter's future partners, and so how I treat Anna might just form their expectations of how they will be treated themselves and it's my job to set the bar high.

So I'll keep making cups of tea, however infrequently Anna chooses to drink them, and have no shame in leaving her to have the last word when her word is funnier than mine. I'll not shy away from public pecks, hugs and pats on the bum. I'll try and show kindness in response to her occassional grumps and resist the urge to shout, snap or snark when faced with those tiny moments of unintentional marital provocation. They'll see me make dinners and do bath times, and usher them away so Anna has space when she needs it to work or sit idle.

And besides, I'm looking forward to having her to myself again once they've both moved on, and I want her to look forward to that day too.

What I think I should hide from my daughters

All the bad things, of course, but then perhaps they need to know a little about famines and terrorists, bigots and burglars, so the world doesn't come as too much of a shock, and it's up to us to manage how they discover these things.

But the biggest thing to hide from them is the low, nagging suspicion that I'm letting them down every single day. Because if allowed to grow, that feeling becomes self fulfilling. The more you chastise yourself as a parent, the more stressed you become about failings both real and imagined, and the more of that they'll pick up on.

The greatest gifts I think a parent can give a child – along with the basics like nutrition, education and some hygeine standards – are self-awareness and self-confidence: to know who they are and to be happy with it.

That, for me, is more important than a straight line of A* test results or a perfectly symmetrical plait.

And if we can manage that, I reckon we will genuinely be parenting the shit out of life.

We'll know for sure in a decade or two.

Good luck!

Moments of Motherhood

(illustrated with bad taxidermy)

What sort of parent will you be?

It will be educational Scandinavian minimalist toys. I also don't believe in ketchup and the iPad.

Do you want this seat?

Yes, yes I do. I needed it 12 minutes 34 seconds ago when you were pretending to be engrossed in your horoscope. I have a 'baby on board' badge. I hate your brogues.

You OK?

Sure. I'm fine. A human has been extracted from my nethers and I seem to be leaking from every orifice but I just feel so blessed.

How was your night?

Is it over? Or has it just started? I'm 74% sure I have been asleep in this position with my eyes wrenched open for some time now. Is it Tuesday? Are we still in the EU?

You hungry?

I use my hands as cutlery and consider fish fingers an amuse bouche.

Thinking of having another one?

I just ate something off my child to save going to the bin, which is 38cm away. I thought it was a raisin. It wasn't. I am also wearing two pairs of undercrackers and consider 2 hours 14 minutes sleep the equivalent of a month in an Ayurdedic spa run by softly-spoken wood nymphs.

Fancy a drink?

Me? You are asking me if there is something I want? Something I need? Something I deserve? I am a person?

What's it like being a parent?

iPad. Ketchup. Peppa Pig. Refusal of the blue spoon in favour of the green spoon, which then doesn't match the pink plate and escalates into a mind-numbing meltdown. Then you find a dribble of wine in the fridge and pair it with a distinctly average microwaveable cottage pie and feel like a culinary overlord.

Acknowledgements

They say it takes a village to raise a child, but it also takes some understanding friends to write a book. We'd like to thank Derek from next door for all the *Incy Wincy Spiders*, Charlotte (@emilygrayphoto) for the endless patience, Linda (@seasonofvictory) and Bryan (bryanmayes.com) for the sparkling designs, Dom, Abi, Lauren, Jess, Sam and all at Gleam for making everything work, Hannah and all at Hodder for their quiet wisdom, the Dam Fam and our London folk for giving us people to eat, drink, laugh and commiserate with, all our families (Cynthia, John, Chris/Dad, Lucy/Mum, Paula/Mum, Andy, El/Sis, Kaz/Sis, Lily and Teddy), the godparents (Pips, Sarah, Tash, Mark, Kaz again, Melissa, Joe and Rob) and podcasters (Natasha, Polly, Noel and Joe again), TENA lady pads, Doug the beagle, Yorkshire tea, cheese, and the inventors of the distilling process. You have all helped in ways we cannot ever repay, but we remain forever grateful.

Do you wish this wasn't the end?

Join us at www.hodder.co.uk, or follow us on
Twitter @hodderbooks to be a part of our community
of people who love the very best in books and reading.

Whether you want to discover more about a book
or an author, watch trailers and interviews, have the
chance to win early limited editions, or simply browse
our expert readers' selection of the very best books,
we think you'll find what you're looking for.

And if you don't,
that's the place to tell us what's missing.

We love what we do, and we'd love you to be part of it.

www.hodder.co.uk

@hodderbooks

HodderBooks

HodderBooks